APHORISMS.

THE MORALIST & POLITICIAN

OR

MANY THINGS IN FEW WORDS

By SIR GEORGE RAMSAY, Bart.

AUTHOR OF "INSTINCT AND REASON," "PRINCIPLES OF PSYCHOLOGY,"
"A CLASSIFICATION OF THE SCIENCES," ETC.

London

WALTON AND MABERLY
UPPER GOWER STREET, AND IVY LANE
PATERNOSTER ROW.

MDCCCLXV.

"At illa altera *Traditio* per *Aphorismos* plurima secum fert commoda, ad quæ *traditio methodica* non attingit. Primum enim de Scriptore specimen dat, utrum ille leviter et perfunctorie Scientiam hauserit, an penitus imbiberit. *Aphorismi* enim, nisi prorsus forent ridiculi, necesse est ut ex medullis et interioribus Scientiarum conficiantur. Abscinditur enim illustratio et excursio; abscinditur varietas exemplorum; abscinditur deductio et connexio; abscinditur descriptio Practicæ: ut ad materiem *Aphorismorum* nihil relinquatur præter copiam observationum bene amplam. Igitur ad *Aphorismos* non sufficiet quisquam, imo de eis nec cogitabit sane, qui se *neutiquam* copiose, et solide instructum ad scribendum perspexerit."—*De Augmentis Scientiarum*, Lib. VI. Cap. II.

CONTENTS.

---o---

PART I.

MORAL AND RELIGIOUS.

	Page
Sundry Moral Aphorisms,	1–39
Contrast between Romanism and Protestantism,	40
Sundry Religious Aphorisms,	42–47
The Metamorphoses of Rome,	48
Dialogue between Romanist and Protestant,	49–57
Romanism, Sectarianism,	57–59
The Church of England,	59–66
The Evangelical and the Rationalistic Christian,	67
Dialogue between Rationalist and Orthodox Christian,	69–72
The DOKETES,	75
The Church militant and triumphant,	76

PART II.

POLITICAL.

Sundry Political Aphorisms,	79–86
The Sovereignty of the People,	87

	Page
The Educational Question,	91
Monarchy; its various kinds,	95
Contrast between Aristocracy and Democracy,	97–103
The use of Party,	105
The Republican Government of ancient Rome; its wisdom,	107
Standing Armies, Militia, National Guard,	108–116
Anarchy, Despotism,	121
On Elections,	124–140
Effects of Centralization and Despotism,	140
Quarrels of Kings and King-makers,	142
What is necessary to a Monarchy, what to a Republic,	143–148
The future of France,	148
Horrors of ancient warfare,	150
The state of Rome under the first Emperors,—from Tacitus,	155–164
The despotism of the Cæsars,	164
The Government of the Three Powers,	164–180
The Federal System,	180–217
The Provincial System,	217–223
The Colonial System,	223
Conclusion: Protest against the partition and spoliation of Denmark,	227

PART I.

MORAL AND RELIGIOUS.

APHORISMS

MORAL AND RELIGIOUS.

———oo———

I.
No desire without fear.

II.
Pain the whetstone of pleasure.

III.
Anxiety, ennui, the Scylla and Charybdis of human happiness.

IV.
The remedy for Ennui is a steadfast desire: for Anxiety there are many palliatives, but no specific, no certain remedy, except it be the absence of desire; and languor from absence of desire may be worse even than anxiety.

V.

How vain, how delusive the opinion of those ancient philosophers who placed Happiness in the possession of some ultimate end! Happiness consists not in standing still, but in progressing. Now, happiness consists in emotion, and desire is a lasting emotion, and essential to progress, while fruition is but momentary. Therefore happiness consists chiefly in Desire.

VI.

If Happiness consist chiefly in desire, may not the desire Benevolence be as good at least as any other? Is it more accompanied with fear or anxiety? No, for the end thereof is not personal advantage. Is its object definite, and its duration necessarily limited? No; its object is infinite, and therefore the desire may last for ever. Is failure here attended with peculiar disappointment? No; even failure is sanctified by the end in view. But the desire is weak. Endeavour then to rouse it into passion. Agreed, but how? By forming an alliance between it and another class of emotions more nearly related to self, and, therefore, more generally interesting; emotions with an infinite object, though not attainable here; which keep us perpetually in pursuit, and prevent the possibility of disappointment or satiety; which may fill the soul with the sweetest satisfaction, or even rouse it into passion. Happy the man whose desires are thus fixed, in whom charity is nursed by religious fervour!

VII.

How much time have you spent in the pursuit of Wealth! how much in the acquisition of Knowledge! how much in the illusions of Fancy! how little in active Benevolence!

VIII.

The force of the desire is measured not by the number of persons benefited, but by the amount of sacrifice submitted to; and it is *pure*, when persons are benefited, not as relations, not as friends, not as private benefactors, not as fellow-citizens, but as *men*.

IX.

Tendency to Self, and more particularly to Sense, tendency to prefer the present to the future, these are the leading propensities which Moral Education is called upon to check. Would you correct in your son an over-weening regard to Self? Accustom him betimes to make sacrifices for others. Words are of little avail, your own example of more, but best of all is his own practice. For Morality is a practical thing, and consists in Habit or Disposition, which is acquired only by use. Accustom, then, your son to do something for yourself as well as for others, and he will continue so to act of his own accord. Parents the most exacting of attentions from their children thus best encourage the social propensity. Why is woman generally less selfish than man? Because she is early taught to make sacrifices of her own time and ease, and is therefore obliged to think of others. Are little children to be taught? who teaches them? a woman. Is any sick? who attends? a woman. Is any afflicted? who consoles? a woman.

X.

Many answers have been given to the question, Why ought I to obey the will of God?

but the true and simple answer is, Because we must suppose that His will is agreeable to the real happiness of mankind. That the real happiness of man is desirable, is a first principle, not to be proved, but self-evident, and therefore whatever tends to that happiness is desirable. Hence moral obligation in general, and in particular the obligation to obey the will of God.

XI.

Life is a race, Desire the goad.

XII.

Man cannot be occupied fully either with the Present or the Past, he must look forward. But in looking forward what does he see? Certainly many intervening objects, but, beyond all, Death closes the scene. How wretched then the condition of man if he must look before him, and must have his prospect bounded by so dismal a spectre! Close then your eyes, endeavour to be thoughtless, chase reflection by the tumult of affairs. But if this be all that human philosophy can advise, the vulgar throng are the best practical philosophers. Agreed.

Is there then no hope for the wise man, no ray of light beyond the tomb. God forbid.

XIII.

"If in this life only we have hope," says the Apostle, "we are of all men most miserable." And the same may be said of men in general as compared with the lower animals. The innocent lamb fears not the butcher's knife until actually applied to its throat, and the patient steer dreads not the hatchet till it falls upon its devoted head. Man alone knows his fate. To console him for that knowledge he has a belief in futurity, a belief that all is not ended here. This belief, however got, is wide spread as the race of man; some philosophers alone doubting or disbelieving, because they cannot logically prove a future life. Such philosophers should therefore be the most miserable of mankind, as their practical advice is the most degrading, for it can consist only in recommending thoughtlessness. Is there then no remedy, must they alone be cut off from the common consolation of mankind? No, blessed be God, who hath brought life and immortality to light through the Gospel.

XIV.

Religious Hope is balanced by Religious Fear. But what desire is unalloyed with Fear? Is Love, Ambition, Covetousness, desire of Fame, Curiosity? And the stronger the desire, the greater the tendency to Fear. But Religious Hope is *peculiarly* liable to Fear. Is it so? Mark that man whose brow is furrowed, whose nights are disturbed, whose days feverish; what secret worm preyeth on his vitals? Is it the dread of judgment to come? Such a dread scarcely flits across his mind. But he has a large stock engaged in trade, he has twenty ships at sea, to-day he is rich, to-morrow he may be a beggar; or perchance he is climbing the ladder of power, and fears to lose his footing. Has the religious man these haggard looks, these restless nights, these anxious days? And if not, how can Religious Hope be peculiarly liable to Fear?

XV.

In Practical Morals it is necessary to distinguish between the *Politic* and the *True*. Half of the discourses one hears, nay more than one half of the discourses on Practical Morality are not strictly true, but politic. If a bow be too much bent in one direction, we may try and bend it in the opposite, but if we succeed, the bow will be broken or useless. So, if mankind be too much inclined to one set of passions, it may be politic to vilify, condemn, and endeavour, as it were, to extirpate them; though to extirpate them would be fatal. What more extravagant than some of the opinions of the Stoics! that to gain or to lose the object of our endeavour, is of no consequence; that life is not preferable to death, and that we ought to despise both; that pain is no evil; and that the welfare of ourselves, of our near relations, of our friends, (if such were possible), and of our country, ought to concern us no more than the happiness of those at a distance. Though these principles be extravagant and impracticable, and would be fatal were they practicable, yet they have produced heroes; and why! Because they oppose certain tendencies of human nature too powerful to be ever destroyed, but adverse to deeds of eminent virtue, while they favour universal Benevolence, naturally a weak desire. Cato, Brutus, Seneca, Marcus Antoninus, all the great and good men who lived in the latter days of the Roman Republic, and the first two centuries of the Empire, belonged to the sect of the Stoics. Still, the *true* is the object of the philosopher, the *politic* of the declaimer; though the declaimer may often be useful.

XVI.

Desire of Superiority the universal Passion.

XVII.

Curiosity, the proper passion of studious men, a solitary passion, apt to decline rather than increase with years, and, of all the self-regarding desires, upon the whole the safest.

XVIII.

"Who cheapens life abates the fear of death," says Young.[1] This is doubtful. Death never appears in such gloomy colours as when we take a melancholy view of this life, for the gloom of our own minds communicates itself

---

[1] *Night Thoughts, N. IV.*

to every object. In cheerful scenes, on the other hand, death loses half its terrors, the cheerfulness of our own minds spreading itself over every subject of reflection, and enlightening even the darkest. With what different feelings do we look upon a churchyard in a crowded city, in the heart of London, and in a pretty village! We approach Pompeii by a street of tombs, but the beauty of surrounding nature, of the earth, the sea, the sky, and the interest attached to antiquity, chase away sadness, or leave only a pleasing melancholy. So, the extreme beauty of the buildings, and the solitary majesty of the desert in the neighbourhood of Cairo, dispel the cloud which might cast a shadow over the tombs of the Fatimite Caliphs. Of all things Nature is most favourable to cheerfulness, and most abates the fear of death.

"The thought of death sits easy on the man
Who has been born and dies among the mountains."[1]

XIX.

It would seem that the near prospect of

---

[1] Wordsworth's *Brothers*.

death should make men thoughtful; and when death is really looked upon as certain, or highly probable, this is generally the case; but when, though near, it is still uncertain, the result is just the contrary. Why are soldiers and sailors, especially during war, reckless, improvident, joyous, and greedy of pleasure? And why, in revolutionary times, do all classes partake of the same rage for present gratification, as was seen remarkably in France during the reign of terror? The reason is that death is ever near yet ever uncertain. Then the Epicurean maxim is reduced to practice, "let us eat and drink, for to-morrow we die:" while the hope that he shall not die, which lurks at the bottom of every man's heart, who lies not under a sentence of death, or who is not worn down by disease, enables him to shake off the dread of dissolution.

XX.

While they who look for no evil fall into real calamities, those who anticipate the worst are tormented with groundless fears. Who shall avoid both? surely his name is *happy*.

XXI.

We may form a pretty accurate estimate of the degree of a person's sensibility from the distinctness with which he remembers the events of his past life. Some, like Mme. Roland, have a perfect recollection of the smallest occurrences from childhood upwards, because they *felt* them strongly; while others, on the contrary, can scarcely distinguish one year from another, for nothing made sufficient impression. To these all years are alike. That Memory depends upon the strength of the original impression, is proved by the well-known fact—that old people remember better the events of their youth, although so remote, than those of recent date. Memory then depends upon the strength of the original feeling; but this may be faint or lively from two causes, the degree of Sensibility peculiar to the temperament, and the presence or absence of any ruling passion, which, by occupying the mind, can prevent it from attending to passing events. Both of these causes contribute to render persons, as they advance in years, more forgetful of the occurrences of yesterday, viz., the decay of Sensibility, and the growth of Ambition, Avarice, &c., which are apt to increase with age.

XXII.

Strange that so many should be employed, not so much in the direct pursuit of happiness as in striving to appear prosperous and happy to others! The reason must be that our self-satisfaction is greatly influenced by the opinion which we suppose others to have of us. Thus the necessity of wealth is forced upon us by the opinion of all around, and with the same command of the necessaries, and even of the luxuries of life, we may feel rich in one country, poor in another. England is a country of Ostentation, France of Simplicity. The prevalence of aristocracy in the former, which is favoured by the right of primogeniture and entails; the system of equality in the latter, which is maintained by the law of equal division, are the principal causes of this difference. In England, (now more than ever), luxury and ostentation run a race.

XXIII.

Some minds are like fire-works,—brilliant

and noisy as soon as lit, but soon ending in smoke and darkness; while others are like the sun, which announces its coming by a feeble dawn, gradually lightens up all the face of nature, then shoots above the horizon, travels on in majesty to the meridian, slowly declines, and though less hot, becomes more mellow and beautiful as it sinks to repose.

XXIV.

Slight is the grief that can brook condolence.

XXV.

Wherein consist our highest enjoyments?— In the exercise of our faculties, mental or bodily.

XXVI.

Can that which leads to *Regret* be really a source of happiness? If you think so, do but consider how permanent a feeling is *Regret*. And is not *Remorse* as permanent but more poignant?

XXVII.

Sentimentality is to real feeling as a bad copy of a picture to the original.

XXVIII.

What is called good fortune or chance is often nothing else than the art of seizing an opportunity. Be quick in seizing your occasion, active in following it up, and your name, like Sulla's, will be the *Fortunate*.

XXIX.

Imagination, the universal Beautifier. What force, even in a trite maxim, when adorned by this Enchantress, as—

> "Weariness
> May snore upon the flint, while resty sloth
> Finds the down pillow hard."

or,

> "The thread of life is of a mingled yarn,
> Good and ill together."

XXX.

Custom, which diminishes the intense, increases the moderate pleasures.

XXXI.

Morning is best suited to *recueillement* or contemplation, because we have not yet been distracted by the world. Sleep gives repose to the mind, separates us from worldly cares and pursuits, and so disposes to reflection. Therefore morning is the best time for devotion,[1] as also for perusing works of imagination, or of reasoning. Gossip of a morning, intolerable!

XXXII.

The recompense for trouble is authority. But I dislike trouble, look not then for Power.

XXXIII.

A taste for amusement, and pleasure in general, makes men agreeable, almost benevolent, where benevolence costs little; while an ascetic life renders them harsh and disagreeable, and even tends to misanthropy: but if this tendency be overcome, creating a habit of self-denial, it prepares for the exercise of Virtue. Why is Youth generally more liked than Age, in other words, why is it more agreeable? Because it has more enjoyments.

---

[1] Hence the importance of early and daily Church service, now happily restored in many parishes in England.

But Youth is not self-denying, and therefore Youth seldom attains to the exalted virtue of mature life.

XXXIV.

Philosophical research, and, in particular, metaphysical inquiry, tends to improve our moral as well as our intellectual state. By fixing the mind on great and general objects, it renders it less subject to the petty annoyances of daily life, and therefore, helps to improve the temper. As a pursuit, the advantage of science consists in this, that it is general.

XXXV.

What is the most dignified of created things? Surely the mind of man. Therefore the philosophy of the human mind is the *philosophia nobilissima.*

XXXVI.

Possibility of change fosters the desire. When we know change to be impossible, we combat any disgust with our present state, otherwise we give way to the feeling. An argument for the indissolubility of Marriage.

XXXVII.

Much of the pleasure of life depends upon a happy mixture of Series and Contrast.

XXXVIII.

Know thyself, said the sage;—but how?—How do you know any thing else? Is it not by observation and reflection?

XXXIX.

Difference between Law and Morals.—There is a wide difference between Law and Morals in the point of view from which they look upon actions. He who frames a Law, puts himself, as it were, in the place of the Deity, the Legislator of the Universe, who acts without passion, and has no respect of persons. So the human legislator constructs a Law, or ought to construct it, without reference to any particular case, but solely with a view to the general good, without prejudice, without passion. His object is the prevention of crime, not vengeance.

Quite different is the position of the practical moralist in the daily intercourse of life. Though it is easy to see that the Purpose or Final Cause of Moral Sentiment is the prevention of Vice, and hence the happiness of the species, yet we must not suppose that the view of that purpose is the main cause which regulates our moral approbation and disapprobation. It is evident that Moral Sentiment must have arisen from its proper causes before the utility thereof could be perceived. But how did it arise? Not from cool calculation and foresight of the general good, but from the view of particular instances of benefit or of injury. Consequently, Moral Sentiment, in its origin, is passionate, and ought to be passionate, or it is good for nothing; for the expression of emotion is its only sanction. We applaud or condemn, not because we have before made up our minds that it is useful to applaud or condemn, but because from the constitution of human nature, acts of beneficence rouse love,—acts of violence, hatred. Therefore the morality of daily life looks not directly to the reformation of society, but to the good or evil of an individual.

From this essential difference between Law and Morals, it often comes to pass that the two are brought into collision, and as Passion is more powerful than cool Reason, so, in the conflict, Morality has the advantage. Thus, upon taking a calm survey of the disastrous consequences of Forgery, and the facilities for its perpetration, English legislators annexed to that crime the punishment of death; but as, in the breast of the moralist, forgery did not excite any very violent indignation, certainly none such as to demand the death of the criminal, therefore that death produced a contrary effect, pity for the object, and wrath against the law and legislator.

To apply this to a peculiar case. It is well known that there are men of sound mind generally, but deranged on a certain subject, and, when under that derangement, capable of the greatest violence, as Bellingham who shot Mr Percival, and M'Naughten who assassinated Mr Drummond.[1] Now the ques-

---

[1] A more recent case is that of Townley who killed Miss Goodwin.

tion is, how are we to treat such persons? In a legal point of view, the question amounts to this: can men of this stamp be restrained from such excesses by fear of capital punishment? We all know that madmen under confinement are governed by fear, can they then be so influenced when at large? But the moral question still remains: will the public bear to see capital punishment inflicted on a man who, at the time he committed a deed of violence, was evidently out of his mind? Will not public sympathy go along with the sufferer, and public indignation be roused against the judge and jury who condemned him, and the legislature who made the law?

According to Law, the greater the temptation the greater the punishment, in order to counterbalance the temptation; but, according to Morals, the more the temptation the less the crime, and therefore, the less the general indignation.

XL.

"Be not solitary, be not idle," a fit conclusion to Burton's *Anatomy of Melancholy*.

XLI.

The secret of success in life: a final *end* constantly in view.

XLII.

Milton's habits: "Up in the morning very early to read good authors." His own words.

XLIII.

Three things necessary to well-being:—*Devotion, Study, Bodily Labour.*

XLIV.

Against three things pray without ceasing:—Indecision, Indolence, Despondency.

XLV.

Great *Readers* seldom great *Thinkers*.

XLVI.

Attention, the parent of Invention.

XLVII.

Sentiment, the creature of Solitude.

XLVIII.

Colloquy: *Psychos.*—"Man is truly man only when he rises above matter." *Hylos.*—"For my part, I like matter." These individuals represent two classes.[1]

XLIX.

Contrast, Contrast, Contrast! Thou soul of enjoyment! thee let me cherish ever.

In a bustling noisy capital how pleasant is a quiet situation, and how enlivening to leave it for the busy streets! Change from town to country, how gratifying! vicissitude of sunny and rainy days, how agreeable! &c., &c. Who would gaze for ever even on the most beautiful object in inanimate nature, a sky without a cloud?

L.

I would give little for a friend who could make a *Catalogue raisonné* of one's defects.

LI.

Surely nothing so invigorates the body as

---

[1] A real colloquy.

the free air of heaven. Therefore air-tight doors and windows, bed curtains, quantities of clothes, all bad.—But I am afraid of catching cold.—I do not deny that in cold countries we may be too much exposed to the air, but we may have fresh air without much exposure, and fresh air strengthens and prevents from catching cold.

LII.

It is easy to turn from Study to Bodily Labour, not so from Bodily Labour to Study. Study requires bodily exercise after it for the good both of body and mind, but bodily labour needs only rest. How many inferences from this proposition! The first part of the day should be given to study; but to the immense majority of mankind this is impossible; therefore the immense majority can never *study;* they may *read* something, but reading is not study.

LIII.

Opinion, the crutch of Virtue.

LIV.

Nothing so absurd as to repine at what you

have freely chosen, and long after that which you have freely given up. Have you selected Wealth or Power for your object? do not regret the loss of your freedom and the want of leisure. Have you fixed upon Knowledge and Literary fame? do not deplore the want of wealth. In every case something must be given up; and if you have had your option, why repine?

So in the choice of a wife. Why did you marry Angelica? She was an heiress, and of a high family. Well, you have got money, you have got connections, why complain that you have not got what you did not seek—a sensible, agreeable, affectionate companion for life?

LV.

"Count," said Pelayo, "Nature has assigned
Two sovereign remedies for human ills:—
Religion, surest, firmest, first, and best,
Strength to the weak, and to the wounded balm;
And strenuous action next."[1]

Lines to be engraven on the heart's core!

---

[1] Southey's *Roderick*.

LVI.

"Subtle as a lawyer, subtle as a Scotsman, subtle as an old man, trebly subtle."[1]

LVII.

Character of a Scotsman:—"Very poetical, very theological, very obstinate, very economical, and very litigious."[2]

LVIII.

Do not suppose that great Virtue any more than great Talent engenders Pride. No; it is a little virtue like a little talent that puffs up. Could Howard have been proud of his philanthropy? But the very regular man often thinks himself very virtuous.

LIX.

For the grief arising from the loss of friends, or from the prospect of our own death, there are but two remedies, Religious Faith and Hope, and Occupation apart from the Grief. The first, if real and lively, is a never-failing

---

[1] French author, anonymous.
[2] Id.

support; the second only a crutch. As for all the consolatory arguments of philosophers, except they go to prove the immortality of the Soul, they are but feeble reeds. But a man in deep grief knows no mental occupation save his grief; he loathes every other. He cannot read, he cannot think of ought else. True, but he may have recourse to violent bodily exercise, and this, accordingly, is the proper medicine for grief, a palliative though not a cure.

LX.

Why did Lord Byron betake himself to boxing when his mother's funeral was moving slowly from the door. Was it from want of feeling or from excess of it? From the latter no doubt. The signs of opposite states of mind may be alike.

LXI.

The pain of grief seems not altogether unmixed with pleasure, otherwise we should not so cherish and brood over our loss. At first, meditation upon the lost object is not only the most natural, but probably the most soothing mental occupation, and therefore, if not excessive, the tendency may be indulged. Is it not good for the mind to experience something of all its possible states? Does not the very principle of change point out that vicissitudes are, on the whole, beneficial, and that a man who could entirely stifle his grief would thereby deprive himself of that rebound of spirits which springs from contrast with the previous melancholy? I have known men who, after a period of deep grief, have experienced even wild spirits such as they never knew before.

LXII.

Grief, when present, is selfish; but the remembrance thereof makes us feel for others.

LXIII.

A warm imagination may supply the place of experience. We sympathise with the woes of others, either because we have felt such woes, or because we can imagine them.

LXIV.

Is not Grief better than Insensibility? Is

it not attended with a secret satisfaction or self-complacency? Is it not better than Ennui, or than the absence of all Emotion? Grief, after all, is a great mental occupation.

LXV.
In deep grief we fly from human intercourse, for the sight of men who cannot feel as we do is hateful. Besides, all deep emotions are reserved! But, in avoiding men, where can we fly? To Self? We are sure to have enough of that. Where then? To Nature, whose sweet presence can beautify Grief, and gild even the tomb.

LXVI.
Nature generally the parent of Cheerfulness, sometimes of Melancholy, never of Mirth.

LXVII.
Mirth, like Laughter, is peculiar to man. It dwells in man, and comes from man.

LXVIII.
Without Religion, without engrossing occupation, frivolity alone can mitigate the fear

of Death. *Vive la bagatelle!* Is not man a noble creature, who, though on the brink of the grave, can be amused with diamonds and spades!

LXIX.

Unhappy the man who has no religion and no frivolity.

LXX.

Custom rather than Reason is opposed to Faith. There is certainly nothing more unaccountable in the Resurrection than in the birth of a human being, nothing in the change against which, in reality, reason can say anything; and though the Resurrection of One at least be established by an immense mass of testimony, yet it is hard to believe what is contrary to common experience.

LXXI.

This hardness of belief is fortified by want of imagination, which, as Butler himself allows, is of "some assistance to apprehension." How then can it be, as he adds, "the author of all error?" So far as it assists apprehension, it must favour truth, and, more especially, a belief in the invisible world. Unbelief in the invisible world may arise from a want of imagination more than anything else.

LXXII.

Comfort, the Englishman's household god. What impiety then to speak one word against it! But, after all, is he not a dull god? For what is his province? Carpets and feather-beds. Who are his ministers? Housemaids. Glorious Apollo, I wish thee joy of thy fellow deity. Oh for an hour of the sun of Delos!

LXXIII.

Many are the mountains of the world, goodly and fair to behold, though they be earthy; but fairy land has few—Parnassus, Cithæron, Helicon, Olympus. O power of Mind, that can build up a heaven upon earth!

LXXIV.

Mont Blanc, the Jungfrau, Chimborazo, fine physical objects; but Olympus is something more, it has a Soul as well as a Body.

LXXV.

Many waters murmur, but thine alone sing, O Castalia!

LXXVI.

A monotonous life is a long day, but a year of vicissitude and feeling is a life.

LXXVII.

Time, like distance, when unmarked, appears nothing. Extreme ease, sleep without dreaming.

LXXVIII.

Sound sleep of a week would seem no longer than one of five minutes. So with a sleepy life.

LXXIX.

Great events are the hour hands of time, while small events mark the minutes.

LXXX.

One passion, one occupation, any one thing cannot mark time, but variety. The face of a clock has many divisions.

LXXXI.

As an expanse of water without shore, island, or rock, so is the life of a quiet man.

LXXXII.

Passions are like storms, which, though full of present mischief, serve to purify the atmosphere.

LXXXIII.

A brooding temper is like a very cloudy day, without wind or rain; but with the electric spark comes the tempest, and with the tempest hope.

LXXXIV.

You complain that time travels fast; why then will you always whip it up? We seem much more afraid of the slowness than of the swiftness of time.

LXXXV.

Impetuous desire would leap over time; Ennui would kill it; Activity values and makes the most of it; the gay neglect, the melancholy alone regret its loss.

LXXXVI.

Both Ennui and Desire would abridge time, but for different reasons; to the one the present is insipid, to the other only inferior to the future.

LXXXVII.

Since activity makes the most of time, it does not regret its flight; but quiet, easy enjoyment feels every day a loss.

LXXXVIII.

Works performed, the only cure for melancholy regret.

LXXXIX.

To some men all days, all years, are alike; to others, each has a character. Does the difference lie in outward circumstances? Only as these affect Sensibility.

XC.

What we have felt, that we remember.

XCI.

If days be marked by variety, and if marked

then felt, the practice of the Church in distinguishing days must be wise.

XCII.

Are not those to be pitied who *feel* not Christmas and Easter?

XCIII.

We admire enterprise, we almost adore heroes in a good cause, we raise costly monuments to their memory, yet we slight St Stephen and St Paul! How consistent are those sturdy sectarians who celebrate the anniversary of the Boyne, and neglect or spurn the anniversaries of their spiritual redemption!

XCIV.

Nothing more agreeable, nothing more beneficial than periodical change, nothing more in harmony with nature. Witness the rotation of the seasons, the sequence of day and night, night and day. Hence the value of the day of rest, and other days of Christian festival.

XCV.

May not this principle be applied more extensively to daily life?

XCVI.

Wise, beneficent Nature! Thou who, in this as in other things, givest us what is good for us without asking our consent!

XCVII.

A very pretty apostrophe no doubt: but an Atheist or a Pantheist might say as much. In poetry this might pass, but in philosophy! You deify the EFFECT, and forget the CAUSE: O wise moralist!

XCVIII.

How I like to confound the *esprit fort*, the minute philosopher! "This is excellent soup, is it not, Marquis.—Excellent.—Do you believe in the cook." [1]

---

[1] Saying reported of Sydney Smith, as addressed to one who had been professing Atheism.

XCIX.

Love is so prone to Jealousy that it is jealous even of the other sex.

C.

Decay of Jealousy is often attributed to increase of confidence, for we are unwilling to allow decrease of Love.

CI.

Love is a commodity the value of which depends entirely on monopoly.

CII.

This monopoly is so strictly guarded, that any foreign article in the least degree similar is prohibited.

CIII.

But when the monopoly ceases to maintain the price, then the prohibition ceases also.

CIV.

Why restrain your wife's intercourse with her female friends? It is surely better than intercourse with men; and do you not see that the one in a great degree prevents the other?—But I would have her content with myself alone.—Then you profess to be both man and woman.

CV.

A love marriage is a risk; but a marriage for money is always a bad bargain.

CVI.

Give me a wife that is a good housekeeper! Why not then a good housekeeper and no wife?

CVII.

A hidden grief is like water pent up, slow, deep, with a muddy bottom; but when the sluice is opened, the stream runs merrily and clears its course.

CVIII.

Delightful Ardour! free gift of Heaven! the soul of life! Who would not sell all and buy thee? But thou art above Price.

CIX.

The ardour of some men dies with their

youth; it is a flash in the pan, a momentary blaze, ending in smoke; while that of others is like the cannon ball—powerful even when spent.

CX.

Scholarships, Fellowships, prizes, medals, honours, goads useful for the herd; but heaven-born ardour can soar without a Tripos.

CXI.

Early distinction not without danger; for sweet but sleepy is a crown of laurels early won.

CXII.

How many, like Atalanta, have been stopped by a golden ball!

CXIII.

Facility prompts the many, Difficulty the few. But even the many care little for that which costs them nothing.

CXIV.

Hence gratuitous education is little valued.

CXV.

Again, Dissenters cling to their conventicle and frequent it regularly, because they pay for the minister.

CXVI.

Free seats in church attract a mass of poor, a changing mass, but those who pay something for their sittings will attend more regularly.

CXVII.

Here Cause and Effect reciprocate. They pay for seats because they mean to attend, and they attend because they have paid.

CXVIII.

Is not the offertory an inducement to attend the Sacrament rather than the contrary? Even the poor man likes to give his penny.

CXIX.

Protestants try to make Religion as easy as possible. The hours of divine service are generally such as to suit the most luxurious habits; churches are made warm and comfortable; no painful vigils, no self-denying fasts, are prescribed. And the more intense the Protestantism, the farther is this system carried. Thus Protestantism endeavours to interest the Soul by indulging the Body.

CXX.

Romanism takes a different line. It well knows the inward satisfaction arising from self-denial and self-sacrifice, and these, accordingly, it promotes by hours of service early and late, by penance and fastings, even by discomfort and cold.

CXXI.

Who is that comfortable man, in a private pew, *sitting* upon a well-stuffed cushion, while the prayers are being read? A Protestant no doubt, who thinks kneeling troublesome, perhaps Popish.

CXXII.

Who is that poor man, with uplifted hands, kneeling on the cold stone? A Roman Catholic you may be sure.

CXXIII.

Which of these presents the finest image of devotion? Which would a painter choose?

CXXIV.

The alliance of Luxury and Religion is bad enough, but it is not so monstrous as that of Religion and Foppery. What have we here? a *fashionable* Chapel!

CXXV.

This is the House of God. Indeed! It looks much more like the house of man. Why, it smells of the world all over.

CXXVI.

This is the poor man's home. Possibly; but meanwhile it is tenanted by the rich.

CXXVII.

How convenient is a term of reproach to put down what we dislike without the pain of argument! Call it Puseyite or Popish and it saves a world of trouble.

CXXVIII.

All true Religion is spiritual. But outward observances do affect the spirit of man. Therefore, &c.

CXXIX.

You acknowledge the divine legation of Moses. But Moses enjoined a multitude of outward observances. *Ergo*, &c.

CXXX.

Jesus Christ himself enjoined outward observances,—Baptism and the Holy Communion. Therefore, again, &c.

CXXXI.

Without some outward observances there might be private piety, but there could be no public worship. And how long would private piety survive public worship?

CXXXII.

Those who are most opposed to outward religious observances yet keep one most scrupulously, even to superstition,—the Sabbath. They resemble the Pharisees of old, to whom our Lord addressed his reproach, "The Sabbath was made for man," &c. Why this scrupulosity? Because it is their only observance, and men cling to it as fathers to an only son. If a passion be natural, the more concentrated the stronger.

CXXXIII.

Therefore, even they who most decry observances *feel* how necessary they are.

CXXXIV.

Outward observances are dangerous, because men are apt to rest in them. But the want of observances is more dangerous, for it leads to indifference or extravagance, to irreligion or fanaticism.

CXXXV.

If a multitude of observances may be thought to supersede good works, so may one strictly kept. What fasting and praying, washing of cups, tithes of mint, anise, and cummin, and the Sabbath, were to the Pharisees of old, that is the Sabbath alone to many a modern sectarian.

CXXXVI.

Pharisee: "I fast twice in the week, I give tithes of all that I possess." Yes, but whatever your aged parents require, that you say is *corban* or dedicated to God. *Sectarian:* "Do I not keep holy the Sabbath day?" True, but you let your old mother go to the workhouse.

CXXXVII.

How the same things do come back again under different names!

CXXXVIII.

Men are glad of any excuse for the non-performance of good works. Outward observances serve the purpose for some, Faith for others.

CXXXIX.

Good works, it is said, puff men up. Do they indeed? Did you ever hear of a very benevolent man who was proud of his benevolence? There is a feeling of satisfaction which attends upon works of charity, but it is not pride, nay, it excludes pride. Charity is too sound a thing to want any false support.

A hale man requires no crutch.

CXL.
But to things of doubtful worth Pride gives a fictitious value; to outward observances and barren states of mind, for we feel that they require puffing.

CXLI.
Tell me which is worst? The pride of Spirit or the pride of Form?

CXLII.
Difference between the Roman Catholic and the Sectarian devotee: the former is humble, the latter proud.

CXLIII.
The Roman Catholic is humble because he has been taught to bend to authority in all religious matters: the Sectarian is proud because he has been taught to spurn authority and rely upon his own judgment.

CXLIV.

Does not the Christian religion constantly enjoin Humility and deprecate Pride? So far, then, Romanism has the advantage of Sectarianism.

CXLV.

But the humble and submissive will be imposed upon so long as men are men, and thus religion will degenerate into superstition. Were priests gods, and the Church a council of gods, Romanism would be perfect.

CXLVI.

If the price be religious corruption, even Humility may be bought too dear.

CXLVII.

That mankind is governed by names is almost a truism. Call the Church a collection of men, and who would believe it infallible?

THE METAMORPHOSES OF ROME.

CXLVIII.
Give place ye alchymists; ye pretend only to change base metal into gold, but Rome changes the fallible into the infallible.

CXLIX.
Prometheus, who of clay made a man, was very bold, nay, impious; but Rome is more bold, more impious, for of a man she makes a god.

CL.
Prometheus stole only fire from heaven to give life to his clay; but Rome has stolen an attribute of Deity.

CLI.
In doing this she has done even more; she has conquered metaphysics; she has separated an Attribute from its Substance.

CLII.
Nay, she has overcome Nature, she has changed bread into flesh.

CLIII.

O Rome republican! O Rome imperial! What are all thy exploits to these? down with thy fasces, off with thy purple, and kneel to Rome the papal.

DIALOGUE BETWEEN ROMANIST AND PROTESTANT.

CLIV.

Protestant.—Rome has exchanged her temporal for a spiritual supremacy, which she fain would impose upon all the nations of the earth. On what are her pretensions founded?

CLV.

Romanist.—You allow that St Peter was an apostle. *Protestant.*—Certainly.

CLVI.

Romanist.—He was not only an Apostle, but the chief of the Apostles.

Protestant.—I find not that anywhere stated in Scripture. St Paul claims for himself peculiarly The Apostleship of the Gentiles,[1] that is, of all nations except the Jews, and to judge from what we find recorded in Scripture, he was a much more stirring apostle than St Peter. Moreover, we find him actually calling St Peter to account for his indecision on a certain occasion.[2]

CLVII.

Romanist.—St Peter received a special commission from our Lord to preach the Gospel.

CLVIII.

Protestant.—St Peter may have received a special commission, but it was not an exclusive commission, for the injunction is laid upon all the eleven Apostles, "Go ye into all the world and preach the Gospel to every creature."[3] "Go ye, therefore, and teach all nations."[4]

---

[1] Gal. ii. 7, 8. [2] Gal. ii. 11, 12.
[3] St Mark, xvi. 15.
[4] St Mat. xxviii. 19; see also St John xx. 21.

CLIX.

Romanist.—To St Peter, expressly, was committed the power of the Keys, and on him especially as on a Rock was the Church to be founded.

CLX.

Protestant.—1. That to St Peter expressly was committed the power of the Keys, is no proof that the same power was not given to the other apostles, and the last words of the Saviour before his Ascension, addressed to all the Eleven, make no difference between them: "Go ye into all the world and preach the Gospel to every creature. He that believeth and is baptised shall be saved, but he that believeth not shall be damned."[1]

2. St Peter himself, in his Epistles, claims no greater power than the other Apostles.

2. St Luke, in the Acts of the Apostles, never hints at the superior power of St Peter.

---

[1] St Mark, xvi. 15, 16. See also St John, xx. 23:—"Whosoever sins ye remit, they are remitted unto them; and whosoever sins ye retain, they are retained." These words were addressed to the disciples generally, assembled together after the Resurrection.

4. St Paul expressly affirms of himself that he was not inferior to *any* of the Apostles.

CLXI.

As to the Church being founded on St Peter as on a rock, so it was, for he laid the first stone of the Church among the Gentiles. This might be called a privilege, but we are not told that it conferred any peculiar power. There is then no ground in Scripture for any power in St Peter superior to the other Apostles.

CLXII.

But I will waive this point for the present, and even allow, for the sake of argument, that St Peter was superior to the rest. What then?

CLXIII.

Romanist.—St Peter was Bishop of Rome.

CLXIV.

Protestant.—Even that is a doubtful point; but for the present I grant it.

CLXV.

Romanist.—The Pope is Bishop of Rome, and therefore the successor of St Peter.

CLXVI.

Protestant.—I do not deny that the Pope may be called the successor of St Peter in the character simply of Bishop of Rome.

CLXVII.

Romanist.—As successor of St Peter the Pope inherits all the powers of St Peter.

CLXVIII.

Protestant.—Softly, softly; that is indeed a sweeping conclusion. St Peter was not only Bishop of Rome, but an original Apostle of our Lord; and because the Pope is the successor of St Peter in the See of Rome, you at once conclude that he is his successor in the Apostleship, in all its powers and prerogatives! Was ever conclusion less warranted by the premises? On such miserable reasoning is founded the claim of universal spiritual supremacy!

Thus, allowing all you can require in order

to build up an argument, allowing (contrary to Scripture), that St Peter was chief of the Apostles, and also, (what is very doubtful,) Bishop of Rome, still the inference deduced from these premises is not worth a rush.

CLXIX.

The Apostles appealed, for the truth of their mission, to the miracles which they wrought. Dare the Popes make that appeal? If not, here at least their power is inferior to that of St Peter or any other of the Apostles.

CLXX.

Without palpable miracles there is no satisfactory proof of revelation or inspiration. The Popes work not such miracles; therefore there is no proof that the Popes have any light superior to other men.[1]

---

[1] The Roman Catholics assert generally, that the power of miracles still continues in their Church, and particular instances are referred to from time to time; but it is not maintained that all the Popes have that power, and wherever the power fails, there fails the proof of infallibility. Were it true that miracles have been performed by certain persons, members of the

CLXXI.

Romanist.—But there must be somewhere an infallible guide to sacred truth. *Protestant.*—Why?

CLXXII.

Romanist.—Because it is allowed that the Bible does not contain rules for every thing, and that even many passages in it are obscure. *Protestant.*—What then?

CLXXIII.

Romanist.—Can we suppose that God would have given to man an imperfect and obscure Revelation, without providing somewhere in his Church, an infallible interpreter thereof?

CLXXIV.

Protestant.—Do you, worm of the earth, dare to say what God should or would do? So long as we reason on the probable go-

---

Roman Catholic Church, which Protestants deny, yet that would prove nothing in favour of the inspiration and infallibility of other members of the same Church; it certainly would not establish the infallibility of all the Popes.

vernment of God from the specimens of that government which we see in his works around us—so long we stand on secure ground; but the moment we desert that ground, and pretend to speculate on the probable conduct of a Being, all-powerful, all-seeing, and all-good, we enter upon the realms of fancy—we lose ourselves in the trackless air. In order to judge of the probable conduct of such a Being, man should himself have the attributes of Deity.

CLXXV.

We know that God allowed the whole world, except a very small district, to remain in religious darkness for at least four thousand years. We know that he allowed his own peculiar people to relapse continually into idolatry. We know that he allowed the Christian religion to meet at its outset, and for nearly three hundred years afterwards, with a most obstinate resistance from Jews as well as Gentiles. We know that he allowed the Mahometan religion to subvert it in the very place of its birth, and over great part of the East. We know that the greater part of the globe still lieth in darkness, and that, even where Christianity is acknowledged and established, it has many lukewarm friends, many heretics and schismatics, many open or secret foes. In the face of such facts we have no reason to conclude that God intended that the evidences of Revelation should be irresistible, or its doctrines clear as the day. To suppose permanent infallibility anywhere on earth—whether in Pope, Council or Church—is contrary not only to the nature of man, but to all that we know of the moral government of God.

CLXXVI.

Romanism, Sectarianism; religious despotism, religious anarchy.

CLXXVII.

Is there, then, no mean between the two? As well might you say that there is no mean between political despotism and political anarchy. Can no pilot steer between Scylla and Charybdis? Daily ships pass in safety through the Straits of Messina.

CLXXVIII.

"I am of Paul, I of Cephas, I of Apollos." Such is Sectarianism; its essence is personality. I am of Luther, I of Calvin, I of Wesley, I of Swedenborg, I of Irving, I of Tait, &c., &c.

CLXXIX.

What Church do you go to? *Catholic,* (not of necessity Roman Catholic,) "St John's."— And you? *Sectarian,*—" Mr Thomson's."

CLXXX.

Talk to me of the Fathers and the primitive Church! Mr Thomson is a godly man.

CLXXXI.

It is the happy morn, the day of rest, the day of devotion and family union. Breakfast is over, and the independent family is preparing to go to church; mamma and the younger girls to hear Mr Thomson, papa and the eldest daughter to hear Mr Smith, and the sons to hear Mr Brown. And this is the day of family union!

CLXXXII.

But when the family meet again, will they not discuss the merits of the preachers, and give an account of the different sermons for the common benefit? I trow not; it is too delicate a subject. Silence is better than wrangling.

CLXXXIII.

As despotism leads to anarchy, and anarchy to despotism, so Romanism leads to Sectarianism, and *vice versa*.

CLXXXIV.

Crescit Roma Albæ ruinis. So papal Rome on the shivers of Sectarianism.

CLXXXV.

Oh rare moderation of the English reformers, who alone could remember that the old Church was not only *Roman,* but *Catholic!*

CLXXXVI.

Passion pulleth down, but passion alone is but a sorry builder. Any fool can demolish a cathedral, but few can raise a Church.

CLXXXVII.

Cranmer, Latimer, and Ridley, were at once humble and bold; humble, for they did not think themselves wiser than all that went before; bold, for in removing much, they dared to maintain that there might be some good even in Babylon.

CLXXXVIII.

There was as much difference between the English Reformation and that of other countries, as between the Revolution of 1688 and that of 1789.

CLXXXIX.

Oh rare moderation of the Anglo-Saxon! who in Politics as in Religion can reform and not destroy!

CXC.

Happy England, that possesses a free constitution, the mature growth of centuries, and a Church conformable to the primitive times! A Church, Catholic in its creeds, Catholic in its discipline, Catholic in its forms, trebly Catholic.

CXCI.

But this Church is in alliance with the State. True; and so was the primitive as soon as the State became converted. The Emperor was the Head of the Church, as now the Queen.

CXCII.

Moreover, if the Church be not in alliance with the State, it will be in opposition. The Civil and the Ecclesiastical powers will be ever at variance.

CXCIII.

But the Church of England is subject to the State. Certainly; for two powers, each claiming sovereignty, cannot co-exist; one must be supreme. So you must choose between Civil and Ecclesiastical rule.[1]

CXCIV.

May they not be closely united in one?

---

[1] In England the supremacy of the Civil Power was established by the Constitutions of Clarendon in 1164. This was the great act of Henry II.

Yes, where the chief magistrate is also High Priest, as the Asmonœan princes, the Caliphs of Bagdad, and the Popes of Rome.

CXCV.

In this case, and in this alone, the spirit as well as the form of the government becomes decidedly ecclesiastical, and the State is absorbed by the Church, rather than the Church by the State.

CXCVI.

In any other case of supposable union the result would be the contrary, the temporal spirit would prevail, and in the fusion the Church would disappear.[1]

CXCVII.

Therefore the true position of the Church is separate, and independent within certain limits, but subject, ultimately, to the State.

---

[1] It is well known that the late Dr Arnold held opinions favourable to the complete fusion of Church and State.

CXCVIII.

For we must never forget that the Church is but a collection of men, and therefore, like the State, fallible. To say that Christ or God is Head of the Church is of no practical avail, unless you pretend, with the Roman Catholics, that he has an infallible vicegerent on earth.

CXCIX.

But the Church of England is the slave of the State. Does a slave enjoy property? Does a master take counsel of a slave? Do slaves have laws and customs which the master dares not infringe without the slave's consent? Show me the Cabinet Minister who dares propose, or if he propose, can carry any important measure affecting the Church, without the approval of the heads thereof, and I will allow that she is a slave.

CC.

Did the Church hold no property; were all her ministers appointed, paid, and liable to dismissal at pleasure by the State; could all her usages be changed without ceremony,—

then she would indeed be the mere creature or slave of the Civil Power. But such is not the Church of England.

CCI.

True it is that the Church of England has now no peculiar Legislature, no Convocation, no general ecclesiastical Assembly. This certainly deprives her of much power, but it is no proof that none is left to her! Nay, it is exactly because she has so strong a hold upon the people, and therefore so much power, that the State is afraid to give her more. The State is not jealous of the Wesleyan Conference, nor yet of the General Assembly of the Church of Scotland, which represents but a poor Church, and a small part of the United Kingdom,—sits only for ten days in the year, and, moreover, is a mixed assembly, consisting of Clergy and Laity, the latter being a large minority. But a Convocation of the Church of England, sitting in Westminster side by side with the Parliament, would be a formidable rival.[1]

---

[1] Since the above was written, an attempt has been

CCII.

The Church of England, with its numerous branches in the colonies, and the sister Episcopal Churches of Scotland and of the United States, is the true mean between Romanism and Sectarianism, and the hope of reformed Christendom.

CCIII.

Where should the doubting Romanist fly? To Calvinism, Revivalism, Quakerism, Unitarianism? To a sect whose creed is Necessity, and whose God a tyrant? or to one that rants and cants; or to another which spurns all

---

made, and is still making, to revive the Convocation. Every good Churchman must allow that some reform is needed in the Constitution of the Church of England, some more ready means of maintaining ecclesiastical discipline. In this respect a lesson might be derived from the Presbyterian Church of Scotland, which, in its Kirk-Sessions, Presbyteries, Synods, and General Assemby, has a complete Ecclesiastical Constitution. Compare this with the delays, uncertainty, and enormous expenses of the Ecclesiastical Courts of England, and, to say the least, the very questionable constitution of the Supreme Court of Appeal, the Judicial Committee of the Privy Council.

Sacraments; or to a fourth which mutilates the Gospel and degrades the Saviour?

CCIV.

Thanks be to God there is yet a Church, Orthodox in its creed, Apostolical and orderly in its discipline, engaging in its forms. Turn hither then O sceptical Romanist, here your soul will find consolation without the sacrifice of your intellect.

CCV.

To this Church may properly be applied those noble lines which Dryden intended for the Church of Rome:—

> "A mild white hind, immortal and unchanged,
> Fed on the lawns, and through the forest ranged;
> Without unspotted, innocent within;
> She feared no dangers, for she knew no sin;
> Yet had she oft been chased with horns and hounds,
> And Scythian shafts, and many winged wounds
> Aimed at her heart, been often forced to fly,
> And doomed to death, though fated not to die."[1]

CCVI.

Christianity has had many foes; some open,

---

[1] *The Hind and the Panther.*

some concealed, some without, some within. Without she has had Jews, Pagans, Heathen Philosophers, Mahometans, Deists, Sceptics, Atheists; within, Heretics, and, now-a-days, Rationalists.

CCVII.

I like not presumptuous epithets. Such are Rationalist and Evangelical, which set up an exclusive claim to Reason and to the Gospel.

CCVIII.

It is a cunning device to hit upon a term which implies approbation, for you cannot say a word against it without an apparent contradiction.

CCIX.

If Rationalism mean the right use of Reason, and Evangelism the true faith as contained in the Gospel, who could gainsay them? To approve, is a truism, to oppose, a contradiction.

CCX.

But these are only open and etymological

meanings, the hidden and real meaning being different; though the etymological meaning be used to make the other pass current, as good money is first put forward that the bad may be taken.

CCXI.

As Evangelism means a peculiar system of doctrine, which the holder assumes to be alone in strict conformity with the Gospel; so Rationalism signifies a peculiar mode of interpreting Scripture, which is assumed to be alone agreeable to Reason.

CCXII.

Consequently, unless Evangelistic and Rationalistic men be infallible, we may attack either system without attacking either the Gospel or Reason.

CCXIII.

All Christians acknowledge the Gospel, and all, even the Roman Catholics, appeal to Reason, for they attempt to prove by reasoning that the Pope or the Church is infallible. That point gained, Reason no doubt must be silent for ever. It is a hard and tough morsel, but you can digest anything after it. Reason, however, is first employed to prove that the morsel is digestible.

CCXIV.

All Protestants, at least, agree that Reason is necessary to appreciate the evidences of Christianity, and to determine what credit is due to the Record. Therefore, ultimately, Faith is built on Reason; and this is the case with no other religion, past or present. It is the exclusive glory of Christianity. No other religion has evidences. So far Christianity is rational.

CCXV.

The Revelation once proved, the accuracy of the Record established, you are bound by Reason to admit the contents *whatever they may be*, for it is a first principle that GOD cannot lie.

CCXVI.

Rationalist.—I will believe nothing that is contrary to Reason.

CCXVII.

I do not wish you to believe anything contrary to Reason; to Reason I appeal as the ultimate tribunal.

CCXVIII.

Rationalist.—Some of the doctrines of the Gospel are incomprehensible, and I cannot believe what I do not understand.

CCXIX.

Every thing in us and around us is incomprehensible; and yet we believe a great deal.

CCXX.

Rationalist.—Some of the doctrines of the Gospel are absurd, as the Incarnation.

CCXXI.

No more absurd than the union of the human soul and body. This we are used to, and therefore it strikes us not with wonder; but on reflection it appears an union of things as different, as irreconcileable as GOD and

Man. "As the reasonable soul and flesh is one Man, so GOD and Man is one Christ."[1]

CCXXII.

Rationalist.—But some of the doctrines of the Gospel are contradictory, as the Trinity.

CCXXIII.

You believe in the union of the soul and body. Now the soul as a spirit can exist in no place. But the soul being united to the body must exist in the same place. But it exists in no place. Therefore it does and does not exist in place. Is the doctrine of the Trinity more puzzling than this? has it more the air of contradiction? Again, two bodies which continually approach must at last meet. But the Asymptote is a line, which, though always getting nearer and nearer a certain curve, never meets it. You cannot swallow this contradiction. Then you must discard Mathematics from the list of Sciences. The Christian Religion may be satisfied if it stand or fall with demonstrative reasoning.

---

[1] *Athansian Creed.*

CCXXIV.

Allow then that your Rationalism is very sorry reasoning. Once allow a divine Revelation, and nothing short of a rigid demonstration can upset any of its doctrines. Will any one pretend to demonstrate the falsehood of the Incarnation or the Atonement?

CCXXV.

Christianity has no *juste milieu*. It is either true altogether, or false altogether. I can conceive either of these alternatives; but what I cannot conceive is, that out of a Divine Revelation any one should have the presumption to take or discard this or that in the name of Reason. Such is the false philosophy against which the Apostle warned his favourite disciple; it is folly in the garb of wisdom, pride shrouded in sophistry.

CCXXVI.

Corruptio optimi pessima. What follies in the name of reason and philosophy! Was ever creed of ignorant savage as absurd as Pantheism? Frightful are the revels of reason run mad. "Nihil tam absurde dici potest, quod non dicatur ab aliquo philosophorum," says Varro. "Oken," says Sir William Hamilton, "intrepidly identifies the Deity or Absolute with Zero.[1] GOD he makes the Nothing, the Nothing he makes GOD."

CCXXVII.

Thus pure reason may terminate in pure nonsense. There is but one science of pure reasoning—the Mathematics.

CCXXVIII.

Instinct, Intellectual Instinct, is a vulgar commodity, yet it acts as a charm against the revels of pure reason. Follow pure reason, and you ought, with Berkeley, to disbelieve the existence of Matter; you ought to doubt your own free will, nay, your own identity.

CCXXIX.

To reject Christianity is a very great mistake, but to metamorphose it is presumptuous and absurd.

---

[1] *Discussions on Philosophy*, Article I.

CCXXX.

They change the thing and retain the name. Is this to deceive themselves or others? I have heard the doctrine of St Simon called a new form of Christianity. Rationalists would probably be horrified if you classed them with Unitarians. Formerly there were Free-thinkers, but now we have free thinking Christians!

CCXXXI.

The form and titles of the Roman Republic long survived its spirit. So in France under the Empire. These professing Christians remind one of the French coins, having on one side *République Française*, and on the other *Napoléon Empereur*.

CCXXXII.

This hypocrisy is still an homage, in the one case to Christianity, in the other to Republicanism.

CCXXXIII.

Augustus, though undisputed master of the Roman world, dared not for his life call himself *Rex* or King; he was only *Imperator*, a well-known military title. So with many Sophists. They are not Infidels, only rational Christians.

CCXXXIV.

Some there are, calling themselves Christians, who deny the reality of miracles, and if so, the Resurrection of Christ. They remove the key-stone, and yet say that the arch may stand: delusion or hypocrisy. That stone gone, there remains only a heap of goodly ruins, interesting to the antiquarian, but nothing more. What name shall we give to these?—An ancient name, the *Doketes*.

CCXXXV.

In the last century, the foe marched up boldly to the city walls under his own colours, because the garrison was remiss; now he seeks an entrance through the gates by hoisting a false flag.

CCXXXVI.

Tactics must be changed to suit the occasion: at one time force, at another subtlety.

CCXXXVII.

The city stands firm for all that, and even extends her borders far and wide, though there be dissensions within, though there be a secession to *Mons sacer*.

CCXXXVIII.

While High and Low strive together at home, Hindoo and African bow to the sign of the Cross.

CCXXXIX.

As the bloody feuds between Marius and Sulla, Cæsar and Pompey, staid not the conquests of the Republic; so the civil war between Romanist and Protestant bounds not the Kingdom of Christ.

PART II.

POLITICAL.

"Quand un peuple a detruit dans son sein l'aristocratie, il court vers la centralisation comme de lui-même."

" Il faudra regretter toujours qu' au lieu de plier cette noblesse sous l'empire des lois, on l'ait abattue et deracinée. En agissant ainsi, on a oté à la nation une portion necessaire de sa substance, et fait à la liberté une blessure qui ne se guèriva jamais."—*L'ancien Régime et la Revolution*, Liv. II. Ch. v., et Liv. II. Ch. XI., par Alexis de Tocqueville.

POLITICAL APHORISMS.

I.

MAN, by nature, says Hobbes, is in a state of war. This opinion has been much found fault with, but without reason. "For WAR consisteth not in battle only, or the act of fighting, but in a tract of time, wherein the will to contend by battle is sufficiently known."[1] This being understood, the above proposition is established by the most extensive experience. Whether you consult civilized or savage life, the truth thereof is apparent. Wherefore all those laws by which, in civilized nations, persons and property are secured? why these constables, these policemen, these hosts of armed men that now cover the face of Eu-

---

[1] *Leviathan*, Part I. Ch. 13.

rope? Why do you lock and bolt your doors at night, your money-chests and drawers even by day, and within your own house, where are none but your children and servants? "Do you not then as much accuse mankind by your actions, as I do by my words."[1] And this too in a country where the government is strong and wakeful! What, then, if Government were weak, or if none? The French Revolution of July 1830 lasted but three days, and the Government was speedily re-established in the person of Louis Philippe; but what took place during this short *interregnum?* All the game in all the royal forests was destroyed from one end of France to another. Not a stag, not a roe, scarcely a a pheasant or partridge escaped the general massacre. Had the inter-regnum lasted longer, can we suppose that private property would have been more respected? In what state then would the country have been?— Surely in a state of war.

Look now at the middle ages. Every rich man's house was a fortress; no one who had

---

[1] *Leviathan*, Part I. Ch. 13.

ought to lose could travel unarmed. Men were clad in steel from top to toe, and they carried about them the ponderous shield, the sword, and lance. Among the Romans, the same word *Hostis* meant originally a stranger and an enemy.

Lastly, turn your eyes to savage nations. Do we not know that these have only two occupations? WAR and the CHASE? What people so backward as not to have invented arms? Nay, what tribe of barbarians does not carry these always about with them? The arms may be rude as the people who made them, but whether in the form of club, of wooden spear, or of bow and arrows, they are more inseparable from a savage than dress. Surely the author of Robinson Crusoe knew human nature; and why should he make his poor solitary islander start with fear on first perceiving a human foot-mark on the sand, unless man by nature were a foe to every man?

II.

No doubt it is monstrous to say, with Hobbes, that man by nature has a right to every thing; in other words, that previous to the institution of a Commonwealth, there could be no distinction between Right and Wrong, no Virtue or Vice, no Morality; but the practice of savage nations gives a show of probability to the principle. Previous to Civil Society, Social Virtue would be confined almost entirely to the domestic circle; for what more could there be when every man looked upon every other as a foe? The best natural disposition would be neutralized by the consciousness that none could be trusted. Where there is no belief in Virtue, there can be none. If, in civilized states, where Religion and early Moral Education, Public Opinion, and Law unite to curb mankind, we are so often imposed upon, what if all these checks were removed? Our idea, then, of the importance of Civil Government must be prodigiously enhanced, when we consider that it is essential, not only to the security of person and property, but even to the development of every Virtue.

III.

If man, by nature, be in a state of war, and if, in every stage of civilization, his passions for ever *tend* to engage him in actual conflict, then, the grand achievement of Human Intelligence is PEACE. How many centuries of war were employed to raise the fabric of the Roman Empire! What wisdom, courage, vigilance, and perseverance, what union of forces, what vast and complicated machinery, were necessary to maintain a general peace of two hundred and twenty years, by far the longest which the history of the world presents! And when the machinery became clogged, and the moving power grew weak, what a long and dreary period ensued! Compared with the centuries of wars which preceded and followed "the palmy state of Rome," those two hundred years of general, if not perfect, tranquillity, appear but as one blue spot in a cloudy sky, or as a green oasis in the Libyan desert.

IV.

Great and permanent inequality tends to corrupt moral sentiment; and how? by preventing sympathy between the different classes of society; for sympathy is between those who are *alike*. What sympathy exists between master and slave? According to Aristotle, the slave was of a different nature from the master; and, accordingly, in the ancient world the sufferings of the former were little felt or heeded. The patriotic, the humane Brutus, who rode round the walls of Xanthos in flames, imploring the inhabitants to have compassion on themselves, could order his slave prisoners to be massacred at Philippi; and his biographer, Plutarch, could record the fact without a word of disapprobation. Many of the primitive martyrs were, as Gibbon observes, "of servile condition, whose lives were esteemed of little value, and whose sufferings were viewed by the ancients with too careless an indifference."[1] Cleopatra is said to have tried the effect of different poisons upon slaves before she fixed upon the asp; and whether this account be true or not, it shews the morals of the age. The distance even between Noble and Serf was too great to allow of much sympathy, and the murder of the latter could be compensated by a trifling fine.[2] Mme. de Sévigné lived not in a barbarous age, but with such

---

[1] *Decline and Fall*, vol. II. ch. 16.
[2] When some friends of mine were in Hungary in the year 1825, a Magnate shot a Jew who had dunned

coolness and even pleasantry does she write of the cruelties inflicted on the poor peasantry of Brittany, on account of an unimportant riot, that one could suppose her a heartless woman: but far from it; she was an accomplished amiable person, only, as De Tocqueville has well said, "Elle ne comprenait pas ce que c'était de souffrir quand on n'était pas gentilhomme."[1]

V.

Revolutions are bloody in proportion to the opposition which they meet with. Opposition rouses rage in the ruling party, rage leads to violence, violence to rancour, and, if possible, to vengeance in the other party, this again to retaliation, and so on in a circle. Rage at present opposition, vengeance for injuries past,—these are the two causes of blood. The banishment of the Tarquins was unopposed; so was that of the Stuarts in

---

him for the repayment of money; but this atrocious act did not exclude the nobleman from the society of his peers.

[1] "She could conceive suffering only in gentle blood."

1688; and these, at first, were bloodless revolutions; while the dethronement of the Bourbons in 1830 met with a short but bloody resistance. The Spanish Revolution of 1820 met with no opposition, hence no blood was shed. But the English Revolution of 1648 was strongly opposed, and the French Revolution of 1789 much more so; and, consequently, in the former much blood flowed both in war and on the scaffold; while in the latter, heads fell like hail upon the pavement, and myriads of men perished on the field of battle! The French Revolution of 1848 was at first almost unopposed, and therefore the victims were few; but when resistance sprang up, the streets of Paris for five days streamed with blood. The *coup d'état* of December 1851 was effected without opposition, and therefore led only to banishment, not to death; while, a year after, an Emperor was elected with less disturbance than an American President.

VI.

Intestine dissensions, Military power,—the two grand causes of the downfall of Republics.

VII.

The general principle, that the majority of a nation ought to govern, is greatly modified by the poverty and ignorance of the lower classes. The doctrine of the sovereignty of the people is not acknowledged in full, at least is not acted up to any where, except in some of the States of America, and some of the small cantons in Switzerland.[1] But, ought it to be everywhere acted up to? No, certainly not; wherever the mass of the people is too ignorant or too poor,—too ignorant to judge well for the common interest, too poor to resist the seduction of bribes, or influence akin to bribery, on the part of the rich.

Besides, there is another danger arising from poverty, simply as such, without supposing ignorance or undue influence. Although it be unquestionably true that an Agrarian Law, by destroying security of property, must

---

[1] Even where the suffrage is most extensive, women are excluded. The Sovereignty of the People was proclaimed in France at the Revolution of 1848, but the Electoral Law of 1850 considerably limited the application of the principle.

undermine one grand pillar of national prosperity, yet, *for the present*, the poor might be benefited by dividing among them the property of the rich. And the poor seldom look much beyond the present hour. Nay, could it be proved that the mass of the people would not be benefited, even for a time, by such a measure, yet the condition of many now labouring under poverty would surely be improved. And as every one hopes to be of the lucky, this expectation might be enough to set the whole in movement.

If to this danger, arising entirely from the poverty of the people, be added the delusions of ignorance, greatly exaggerating the advantages of a general division of property, and the arts of ambitious men fostering these delusions and inflaming the passions of the multitude, we may well fear that a needy populace, having the *power* of passing an Agrarian Law, would not long want the *will*.

In addressing such a populace, the advocates for an agrarian law would have an immense advantage over their opponents. First appearances are surely in favour of the former, and, what is more, the cupidity natural to man, and to the needy in particular, is on their side; whereas, the arguments of the latter must be drawn from abstract notions of justice, and from remote consequences, and, moreover, will be at variance with the passions of their hearers. Can we then doubt whose reasons will be found the best?[1]

A striking exemplification of the truth of the above remarks is presented by the history of the French Revolution of 1848. The populace of Paris can hardly be supposed to be unusually ignorant, and they are certainly not poorer than the populace of most large cities; but, persuaded by the arguments, and moved by the addresses of designing men, they adopted, with enthusiasm, Agrarian or Socialist doctrines, and proved themselves in earnest by fighting desperately for them. The same history proves that no opinions are too absurd—no schemes too wild to find able supporters, where much may be gained by deluding the people. Men of established reputation, writers of great talent, were not ashamed openly to

---

[1] These remarks were written long before the Revolution of 1848.

profess Socialism;[1] and even a Minister of Public Instruction did not scruple to sound the praises of Ignorance.[2]

VIII.

According to the Mercantile System, all wealth consisted in gold and silver. Hence the grand object of a nation was to amass these, and exportation of all things but these was to be encouraged, importation discouraged, in order that a balance might be due to be paid in the precious metals. This visionary system sank under the genius of Adam Smith; but it was not so soon seen that the effect of the system in amassing gold and silver is imaginary, as well as the advantages thereof. When the exports of a nation exceed its imports, a balance is no doubt due; but how is this to be paid? In gold or silver, is the common answer. Why so? Is the foreigner who has to pay obliged to pay in gold or silver, or will the native merchant who has to receive be satisfied with nothing else?

---

[1] Émile de Girardin, Eugène Sue, and many others.
[2] Carnot.

Can any reason be shown for either of these suppositions? And if no reason can be shown, why are they maintained? Merchants have no predilection for the precious metals, they give or accept them as it suits their convenience at the time, that is, according to the state of the market; and if the foreigner, who has a debt to discharge, find it more for his interest to send a remittance in goods, he assuredly will not send it in gold.[1]

IX.

The Educational Question, which is rather puzzling, may be exhausted thus. When the

---

[1] The Mercantile System began to be acted upon as long ago as the time of the Long Parliament. Hume observes in a note (*History of England*, vol. VI. c. 54.):—" It was an instruction given by the House to the committee which framed one of these bills, (1st June 1641), to take care that the rates upon Exportation may be as light as possible, and upon Importation as heavy as trade will bear,—a proof that the nature of commerce began now to be understood." The opinion of Hume is remarkable, and shows how little *at that time* he was imbued with the principles of his friend Adam Smith. Had he written *misunderstood* he would have been nearer the truth.

State undertakes to provide education for the people, in a country where there is an Established Religion along with a diversity of Sects, that education may be: *First*, either purely Secular or Religious and Secular. But the first of these schemes is disapproved by all sincere Christians of whatsoever denomination, therefore it is excluded.

Secondly, Religion being adopted as an essential part of the scheme, religious education may be in accordance with the Established Church exclusively, or it may be adapted to Christians of all denominations. But the first of these schemes, though agreeable to the Church, would be disapproved by all dissenters, and, consequently, where these are numerous, the intention of the State, with respect to education, in the case of many, would be frustrated; therefore it is excluded.

Thirdly, It being granted that religious education must be adapted to Christians of every persuasion, this education along with secular may be given either in different schools, or in the same school. But, by the first scheme, we waste our means by establishing and keeping up too many schools, and the Church incurs the reproach of directly encouraging dissent from the Established Church. Therefore it is excluded; though it be the present system of the Privy Council.

Fourthly, It being allowed that the religious education of all Christians should be given in one school, this education may be in common or not in common. But the difficulties of the first scheme are very great, when Sects differ widely. A religious education agreeable to the Church would not be agreeable to dissenters, and that acceptable to dissenters would not content the Church. Moreover, could all Protestants agree in a system, still Roman Catholics would be left out, and *vice versa*. Therefore *this* system is excluded, though it be the one adopted by the State in Ireland, where, by means of extracts from the Bible, that is, by garbling, a partial success is obtained, but only partial, for very many of the Church of England keep aloof. It is adapted to Roman Catholics, not to Protestants; and, as in Ireland the former are the great majority, it of course embraces the many but not the few. In a Protestant country, such a system would be inadmissible, for, to please the few, it would materially impair the religious education of the many. The system of the British and Foreign School Society comes under this head, for in their schools the Bible alone, and the whole Bible, is read; by the first of which regulations the children of good Churchmen are excluded; by the second, all Roman Catholics. In Scotland, the system of religious instruction in common has answered well, because the dissenters differ from the Established Church neither in Faith, nor in Worship, only in Church Discipline.

Lastly, It being granted that religious instruction should not be in common, though in the same school, the only remaining scheme is that Religion should be taught apart, at a certain hour or hours, by different masters, whether lay or clerical, appointed by the different sects for this purpose only. This is the system adopted in the great Ragged School of Edinburgh, where Roman Catholic and Protestant children are educated together, and it succeeds perfectly. Though the ordinary masters and the majority of the managing committee are Protestant, yet Roman Catholic children are treated with perfect fairness, for they are instructed in religion within the walls of the school, by teachers of their own Church. Under such a system, the schoolmaster might always be of the Established Church, and ought to be so, because, where there is a choice, the Establishment should always be preferred by the State. If not, why is there any Establishment? But all dissenters should be free to choose another religious instructor for their children, nay they should be obliged to do so if they reject the teaching of the Established Church, otherwise the education, so far as they are concerned, would be purely secular; and this instructor should receive no payment from the State. Thus Church and School would be in harmony, the Establishment favoured, dissenters free, but not encouraged.

X.

Monarchy may be divided into two sorts,—Pure Monarchy or Despotism, and Mixed or Limited Monarchy. The latter again may be subdivided into Feudal or Customary, and Constitutional Monarchy.

XI.

The question,—On what is Government founded? may mean either

(*a.*) What are the forces, the causes, which, *in fact*, maintain government? or

(*b.*) On what is founded the *right* of Government to command, and the *duty* of the people to obey?

The one relates to the foundation of Government *de facto*, the other, *de jure:* In other words, the one is concerned with *What is*, the other with *What ought to be:* The former is a question of Causes, the other of Reasons.

XII.

The question,—Where lies the supreme power in any State? is easily answered in the first instance, In the legislature. But where does it reside ultimately? Who governs the Legislature? To this no general answer can be given, for one State differs from another, and no two are quite alike. The two extremes are Pure Monarchy and Pure Democracy, where the ultimate power is lodged with One, or else with the absolute Majority, but between these there are countless varieties.

XIII.

The sovereignty of the people is not, as demagogues maintain, an ultimate principle; it is dependent on the principle of Utility. From this there is no appeal.

XIV.

Proximate principles are useful, nay necessary, in Politics as well as in Morals, but they are apt to make us forget the Ultimate.

XV.

Monarchy is prompt; Aristocracy close, constant, and wise,—both oppressive; Democracy open, living from day to day, on the whole good-tempered; easily enraged, but easily pacified; incapable of deliberate injury to self; thoughtless, and easily misled.

XVI.

The wars of Aristocracy are wars of calculation; those of Democracy of passion. Of this no more striking instance can be given than the present wretched contest between the Northern and the Southern States of North America. Such a war would never have been carried on, as it now is, by a calculating Aristocracy, for they would soon have seen the conquest and subjection of the South by the North to be impossible. It is a war of pure passion on the part of the North, the passion of dominion, the fear of loss of national grandeur. How mistaken are they who maintain that Democracy is peculiarly pacific! War is not for the interest of the people, but it may gratify their passions.

XVII.

Favouritism is the vice of Aristocracy, Venality of Democracy. The great gains derived from the war by a small portion of the North American people help to fan the flame.

XVIII.

War is a very serious thing,—the result always uncertain; therefore, on the whole, reflection must be against it. Many a blow is stopped by a moment's consideration; many a challenge by a night's counsel.

XIX.

But Passion reflects not, and occasions for

passion never fail. On this account, Democracy is more prone to war than Aristocracy.

XX.

There have been warlike Aristocracies, as the senate of Rome, and, we may add, the Aristocracy of England. But the Government of Rome, like that of England, was by no means a pure Aristocracy, with it the democratical element was largely blended.

XXI.

All the Feudal Aristocracies were warlike, for in semi-barbarous times men take to war and the chase from want of some other occupation. Besides, the Feudal Aristocracies were not so much organized bodies, as a number of separate individuals, each swayed by his own passions.

XXII.

How fond of war was the Democracy of Athens! How prone to it is that of America! In 1793 the Democracy of France poured the tide of war over Europe; in 1848 it convulsed the Continent from the Rhine to the Euxine, from the Baltic to the Adriatic. In 1861 the Democracy of the Northern States of America would have rushed into a war with England, rather than make reparation for an insult, had not the Government interposed. Reason, calculation, would have recommended a peaceable separation of North and South, but Passion was in favour of war. Bentham's boast as to the rising Republic, is, alas! no longer true. The contending parties, says he, used up reams of paper, but shed not a drop of blood. On the other hand, how cautious were the old and long-established aristocracies of Venice and of Bern!

XXIII.

As Aristocracy is more constant, more persevering than Democracy, this difference should appear in the conduct of their wars. Once engaged in war, Aristocracy will not soon give up.

XXIV.

Aristocracy suffers less during the course of a war than the people generally, it has also more to hope from success, and more to fear from failure. No wonder if it be more persevering.

XXV.

Take, as a specimen, the last war in Hungary (1848-9). The Aristocracy (the Magyars) suffered less than the people generally during the course of the War, because they could remove with their effects to any spot; they had more to hope from success, for they looked to political power; and they had everything to fear from failure—confiscation of their property, and death.

XXVI.

What can exceed the tenacity of the Polish Aristocracy? All the evils of war fall without alleviation upon the serfs, and their condition under the Russians may be no worse than under their former rulers; but the nobles have much to gain by success, and all to lose by failure, while the excitement of war compensates them for present privation.

XXVII.

Where the people does not enjoy political,

still more, social freedom, they *may* be none the worse for a change of masters.

XXVIII.

The sure proof of the utter degradation of a people is the want of national spirit.

XXIX.

Miserable must be the condition of a people to whom the loss of political independence is no loss!

XXX.

The People is oftentimes more patriotic than the Nobility; for the nobles may be corrupted, a whole people cannot. So it was in Scotland during the long contest for independence with the three Edwards of England. Many of the nobles, nay Bruce himself at first, were gained over by the English monarchs; but Wallace and the people were always true. At Dupplin, near Perth, the Earl of Athol betrayed the Scottish army to the English; and many other nobles, in particular the Earl of March, were afterwards traitors to their country. So in Ireland. The nobility sold themselves to England for money and rank, the people were sound, but without power; so the Irish Parliament fell. Nobility of Ireland, not all the waters of the Shannon can wash out this stain. It will mark you for ever and ever. Sell your country for pelf! faugh!

XXXI.

The Governments of Europe before the French Revolution were akin to despotism; but in general they had not destroyed national spirit.

XXXII.

In France, in particular, this was always strong, a proof that the old government was not very bad.

XXXIII.

But in the Papal States and in Naples, till of late, there were no national spirit; a proof of the degradation of the people and of the tyranny of government.

XXXIV.

As Despotism destroys, so Liberty creates National Spirit.

XXXV.

Even Self-love may be almost quenched by vice and misery; much more Love of Country.

XXXVI.

If National Spirit be the sure defence of National Independence, and if national spirit be fostered by Liberty, then is Liberty the ægis of Independence.

XXXVII.

Attend to this ye monarchs of Europe, who think that the only safeguard of your dominions is standing armies.

XXXVIII.

Can any thing compensate for the loss of National Independence? Can *Peace* compensate? Compare Greece and Sicily independent, with those countries under the Romans. Compare Samnium independent, with Samnium after the Roman conquest as described by Livy, depopulated, spiritless, and helpless. In spite of frequent wars Greece and Sicily flourished when independent; in spite of peace they languished and decayed under the Roman empire. How does this apply to our dominions in India?

XXXIX.

Much has been written for and against Party: but those who declaim against all party, declaim, in fact, against all combination. Now, without some combination I should like to know what can be done in politics.

XL.

Party may degenerate into Faction, parties of principle may become chiefly personal or selfish; but what of that? Are not all things liable to degeneracy?

XLI.

Without parties in a free state one of two things must happen. Either the Government, in the absence of a combined, that is of an effectual, opposition, will be able to do as it pleases; or if Government itself can form no party, then the reins of power will be changing hands continually. In a word, Government will be either too strong or too weak.[1]

XLII.

What a Babel would be the House of Commons, were every one to speak without consulting and uniting with others! And how could legislation ever be carried through?

XLIII.

Independence is a fine thing, an attractive name; but in political life isolation is useless. Nothing can be *done* without union.

XLIV.

Were every man to follow his whim, there would be neither State nor Church.

XLV.

God stands alone, but man cannot. Woe to him who sets himself above humanity.

---

[1] In 1851, the latter was pretty much the case in England, as well as in France before the *coup d'état*. The subdivision of parties is equivalent to none.

XLVI.

Thought may be free as air, speculation uncontrolled; but, to act together, men must give and take.

XLVII.

The Sectarian who can read his Bible in his own tongue thinks himself wiser than the ancients; but were all men so minded, where would be the Church?

XLVIII.

The old Republican Government of Rome affords grand lessons of political wisdom. Three great principles may be noted:—

First, not to put political power in the hands merely of the greatest number.

Secondly, not to arm the *Proletarii*, or poorest of the people.

Thirdly, not to allow generals to command, and to permit the men to depart, after one year.

XLIX.

The first of these principles is opposed to universal suffrage; the second, to the service of all classes, including the poorest, as militia or national guards. Both principles were violated by the Provisional Government of France (1848). It established universal and equal suffrage, and put arms into the hands of all. The result was soon seen in the five bloody days of June.

L.

The English system of enlisting all the riff raff of society for a number of years is directly opposed to the Roman; but in a Monarchy such as ours, and with an aristocratical body of officers, there is little danger.

LI.

The French conscription for seven years' service, combined with the system of *remplacement militaire*, or that of substitutes, is also opposed to the Roman, for it tends to exempt the rich from military service, and confine it to the poor.

LII.

But the Prussian system, which exempts

none, and limits to three years the period of active service, comes nearer the Roman.

LIII.

Thus Prussia has a Republican army in a Monarchy. Consequently, she submits to the greatest sacrifice required by a Republic,— the sacrifice of three prime years to military service, without the advantages of a Republic.

LIV.

Switzerland has no standing army; but the use of arms is universal, and all may be called to serve the Republic.

LV.

The Romans changed their generals every year. This was favourable to the civil constitution, but adverse to the arms of the Republic.

LVI.

The men were allowed to go home after a year's service. Same observation. When, at last, military command and military service were prolonged, conquests became more rapid, but civil Liberty fell.

LVII.

So long as standing armies were unknown, the best militia would gain the day, but no longer.

LVIII.

The veteran troops of Hannibal easily vanquished the raw soldiers of Rome, though the best militia in the world.

LIX.

The substitution of standing armies for militia, now become a necessity, renders Republics in Europe all but impossible.

LX.

The contest now raging between the Northern and the Southern States of America is on both sides carried on by militia, and they are well matched. Almost all the battles have been doubtful victories on either side, and whether it be the fault of the generals, or of the troops, or of both, success has never been followed up. This equality may prolong the contest indefinitely.

LXI.

The substitution of standing armies for the feudal militia established despotism all over Europe; and the same cause now prevents the growth of Constitutional Government. But these armies saved Europe from Socialism and Anarchy in 1848. Yes; these armies first made Europe unused to liberty and therefore unfit for it, and then repressed its excesses. So that Despotism, as well as the Orgies of Liberty, are all owing to the overgrown standing armies. We do not think ourselves much indebted to the man who simply repairs the mischief which himself has made.

LXII.

The insular position of Great Britain is not only an advantage, it is *the* grand thing without which all other advantages would have been lost. Had England been a part of the Continent, it must have had permanent armies to defend itself, and it would have shared the fate of Europe.

If Charles I. had found or formed an army, he might have become as despotic as Louis XIV. Cromwell with fifty thousand soldiers kept all Britain in subjection.

LXIII.

Charles V. was the great enslaver of Europe, for he first firmly established the modern military system. He destroyed the ancient liberties of Spain, and did all he could to ruin those of Germany and the Netherlands. Protestantism alone made successful head against him.

LXIV.

Had England shared the fate of Europe, where would have been a successful example of free government? And who can estimate the value of such an example?

LXV.

Were Europe threatened by a new swarm of barbarians, standing armies would be the safe-guard of civilization; but Scandanavia, Germany, and Scythia have spent their rage.

LXVI.

Upon the whole, standing armies are the curse of Europe.

LXVII.

This may be true; but where is the remedy? Will all the States agree to disarm? And if one only refuse will it not conquer the rest?

LXVIII.

A general disarmament would be best; but till that take place a check may be found to a standing army in a National Guard or Militia.

LXIX.

As protectors of public order in revolutionary times, a National Militia is little to be relied on, for it changes as the people change, and discusses when it ought to act; but, as guardians of public liberty, a militia may be invaluable. Where the Army is numerous and liberty new, a National Militia is the only effectual check. No wonder if despots hate it.

LXX.

As an Army is a defence against foreigners,

so is the Militia against the army. The one protects National Independence, the other Civil Liberty.

LXXI.

Consequently, in the present state of continental Europe, nothing is so important as the organisation of an efficient National Guard. It is the one institution necessary for the security of every other.

LXXII.

What England owes to the sea, Switzerland owes to the Alps. Strong in these bulwarks and in her excellent militia, she can dispense with a permanent army. Happy the country where a Republic is possible.

LXXIII.

How much is implied in that possibility! What virtue! what absence of misery on a great scale!

LXXIV.

What would our lawyers, our physicians, our bankers, our merchants, our tradesmen think, were they called upon at a moment's warning, deserting their clients, their patients, their country houses, their shops, to shoulder a rifle and be off? But for this the Swiss are always prepared. Such is Republican virtue.

LXXV.

Happy the country whose greatest cities are Geneva and Bern.

LXXVI.

Happier still the country where the peasant has his cottage and his land.

LXXVII.

Happy above all the country which can say, A Republic is here a reality.

LXXVIII.

As England has shown that a Monarchy may be free, so Switzerland has proved that Republics are not confined to Eutopia or Oceana.

LXXIX.

The force of an army increases in a far greater ratio than its numbers, at least up to a certain point, when numbers become unmanageable. An army of 20,000 men is more than twice as powerful as one of 10,000. But any popular force does not increase even in proportion to the number of the people, for it is lost by dissemination. It is only in great cities that it becomes formidable, as in Paris or Lyons. Consequently, the army in a great country may bear a far greater ratio to the available popular force than it can in a small one. Therefore military despotism is much more easy in large than in small states. It becomes very difficult, almost impracticable, for any length of time, in small states such as the Republics of ancient Greece, and of Italy during the middle ages. The longest of Grecian despotisms, those of Pisistratus at Athens and Dionysius the Elder at Syracuse, were upset in the next generation.

LXXX.

Hence we may judge of the wisdom of those democrats who wished to fuse all Germany into one. The sub-division of states is much more favourable to liberty. Had the Duke of Nassau been left to his own resources in 1850, he must have submitted to his people. Nothing could be more adverse to the liberties of Germany than the admission of Austria *with all her states* into the Confederation.

LXXXI.

How often do we hear it said, Such a people is not fit for liberty. This may be, but what then? If we wait to give them liberty till they be fit for it, we may wait for ever. Unless they make trials they never can be fit. Political Education is not the work of a day; the beginning must always be difficult and often dangerous. Shall we therefore always cling to despotism?

LXXXII.

The misfortune is that men will run into the opposite extreme. The more unfit they are for Liberty, the greater the dose which they attempt to swallow. Thus in 1848, nations utterly unaccustomed to self-government would be content with nothing short of universal suffrage! These political novices looked contemptuously on the freedom of England! Lords and Commons, Bah! an antiquated system, good enough for the days gone by. Now we will shew them something better,— the Frankfort Parliament.

LXXXIII.

A Republic in Hungary! the climax of absurdity.

LXXXIV.

Oh Opportunity! were I a polytheist I would worship thee. But thou art a slippery god, once let go in vain we try to catch thee.

LXXXV.

If Louis the XI. of France had married Mary of Burgundy he would have given to France the barrier of the Rhine for ever. If in 1814, nearly three hundred and forty years afterwards, Napoleon had agreed to the terms of the Allies before they crossed that river, this long desired barrier would at last have been gained. When will such opportunities come again?

LXXXVI.

One could weep to think how the opportunities of 1848 were thrown away.

LXXXVII.

As yet (1851) there is but one result on which one can look with satisfaction,—the establishment of a constitutional government in Piedmont with some prospect of success. If it do succeed it will inoculate all Italy.[1]

LXXXVIII.

"*Il n'est bon de se déshabiller avant de se coucher,*"[2] said to me once an old Swiss peasant. King Lear might have learned wis-

---

[1] I leave this as I wrote it in 1851. The result has exceeded my most sanguine expectations. But in 1848, Austria being hard pressed on all sides, a grand opportunity was lost. Charles Albert, having overrun Lombardy, might have had the barrier of the Mincio, which only was got eleven years afterwards by French intervention and another bloody war. How much better had it been owing to national efforts alone! On these two occasions the conduct of Carlo Alberto and of Napoleon III. were exactly opposed, the one being contrary, the other agreeable to the wise policy of the Romans in their early wars, so much praised by Machiavelli, namely, to be content with a decided advantage, not to drive the enemy to despair, and to make peace as soon as possible.

[2] It is not good to strip before bed time.

dom from such an one, and even our Henry II. who, though a very able prince, showed not his wisdom in this, that he made his sons too great in his lifetime. Accordingly, they rebelled against him, and embittered all his latter days.

LXXXIX.

Strange that the ablest politicians should sometimes make the greatest mistakes. Thus Henry II. made Becket Archbishop of Canterbury, and gave principalities to his sons while he still lived and reigned. Yet Becket was no stranger to Henry, he had been his Chancellor and even his friend. What a mistake in Napoleon was his march to Moscow instead of restoring Poland!

XC.

Caracalla gave the freedom of Rome to all free subjects of the Empire. This was a cause of its decline. Before his time the Roman citizens formed a privileged class, spread all over the Empire, and had as such, a *peculiar interest* in the prosperity and grandeur of Rome. They were a sort of Aristocracy, and were a support to the empire on the same principle as an Aristocracy supports a throne.

XCI.

Anarchy as long as it lasts may be worse than Despotism; but fortunately it cannot last long: whereas Despotism is eternal.

The revolutionary orgies of France—the Reign of Terror, reckoned only by months; but Despotism counts by centuries.

XCII.

Here what one despot did, one out of very many. "It was computed that under the vague appellation of the friends of Geta, above twenty thousand persons of both sexes suffered death by order of Garacalla."[1] Again, the same emperor ordered and witnessed a general massacre at Alexandria. And to think that such a government should last!

XCIII.

Alluding to the election of the Emperor

---

[1] Gibbon's *Decline and Fall*, Vol. I. Ch. VI.

Jovian, Gibbon says:—" In a government which had almost forgotten the distinction of pure and noble blood, the superiority of birth was of little moment."[1] Thus despotism and extreme democracy meet. The result of both is the same—Equality; and this result facilitates despotism in both cases.

XCIV.

Julius Cæsar was never thought cruel, nay, he was celebrated for his clemency: yet mark with "what indifference he relates in his *Commentaries of the Gallic War, that* he put to death the whole senate of the Veneti, who had yielded to his mercy, (III. 16); *that* he laboured to extirpate the whole nation of the Eburones, (VI. 31); *that* forty thousand persons were massacred at Bourges by the *just* revenge of his soldiers, who spared neither sex nor age," (VII. 27).[2] Remember also his treachery towards the Usipii and Tencteri, (IV.); and his cutting off the hands of his

---

[1] Gibbon's *Decline and Fall*, Ch. XXIV.
Id. Ch. XXVI. *note.*

prisoners taken at Uxellodunum, (VIII. 44). And this man was praised for his clemency! What a satire on the age is that praise!

XCV.

Constantine was the first Christian Emperor. How many enormities have been covered by that fact! We forget that he put to death his father-in-law Maximian, his brother-in-law Licinius, and probably his wife Fausta.

XCVI.

The following account of the plan of defence adopted by the Persians when their country was attacked by Julian, might serve for a description of the Russian mode of warfare against Napoleon in 1812. "Wherever they moved, the inhabitants deserted the open villages and took shelter in the fortified towns; the cattle were driven away; and the grass and ripe corn were consumed by fire; and as soon as the flames had subsided which interrupted the march of Julian, he beheld the melancholy face of a smoking and naked desert. This desperate but effectual method of defence can only be executed by the enthusiasm of a people who prefer their independence to their property; or by the vigour of an arbitrary government which consults the public safety, without submitting to their inclinations the liberty of choice."[1]

XCVII.

When treating of the means employed to establish a democracy, Aristotle says, "Every expedient will be employed to melt into one great whole the different classes of citizens; all former associations will be suppressed."[2] What a correct picture of the French revolutionary movement!

ON ELECTIONS.

XCVIII.

Both Machiavelli and Montesquieu maintain that the people is admirably fitted for the business of election; and in proof of this they refer to the succession of eminent men chosen

---

[1] Gibbon's *Decline and Fall*, Chap. XXIV.
[2] *Politics*, Book VI. Chap. IV.

at Rome and at Athens. Let us examine this opinion.

XCIX.

Those who have paid particular attention to any subject are more competent to elect a Head connected with it than men in general. This will not be disputed.

C.

Where many have paid particular attention to any subject, they will *in general* be better qualified to elect a Head in that line than any individual.

CI.

For, (*a.*) If an individual be the elector, what security have we for *his* fitness? If he elect by right of birth, then we can have none; and if he be deputed by another, who will answer for that other?

(*b.*) Individuals are subject to eccentricities of opinion to which a body of men is not liable; for in a body different eccentricities neutralize each other.

(*c.*) Individuals have their friends and favourites.

(*d.*) They are more open to corruption than a numerous body. Under this head is included all the sinister interest of an individual.

(*e.*) They are free from debate and opposition, and therefore their errors find no correction.

(*f.*) Therefore, *cæteris paribus*, many electors are preferable to one.

CII.

We have thus determined two elements of good election; knowledge, special knowledge, and numbers.

CIII.

This being so, the more we can enlarge the numbers without losing the other advantage the better. But there is the limit. We must combine both advantages, not sacrifice one to the other.

CIV.

Thus, to choose a Judge, the lawyers would be the best electors; to choose a Head Physician or President of the College, the whole body of physicians; to choose a Bishop, the clergy; to choose a General, the officers at least, if not the men. In Glasgow College the best student is declared by the votes of his fellows, and they generally choose aright. In all these cases we have what we want, a number of well-informed electors.

It is evident that on such subjects the public in general is not well informed; and therefore incompetent. By admitting them to vote we should lose more by their want of knowledge than we should gain by their numbers.

CV.

On the same principle, the members of an aristrocratic chamber, who have studied politics all their lives, are better qualified to name a Minister of State or a Diplomatist than the mass of the people. On the principle of numbers, they are also better than an individual. Therefore the Constitution of the United States has wisely provided that the appointment of the highest functionaries, diplomatic and judicial, should lie with the President *and* two-thirds of the Senate, neither with the President alone nor with the House of Representatives.

CVI.
In point of intelligence, an aristocracy is most competent to elect Legislators also; but here it fails for want of sufficient numbers.

CVII.
In point of numbers, the whole body of the people is best of all; but it lacks knowledge.

CXVIII.
Therefore some middle system is preferable, some combination which shall unite sufficient knowledge with sufficient numbers.

CIX.
There are then two principal questions, What knowledge is necessary for an election? and in what body sufficiently numerous shall we find it?

CX.
In local affairs, parochial or municipal, a very limited knowledge is necessary, and of a

kind which each member of the parish or borough is likely to acquire, if he acquire anything, because it nearly concerns himself. Therefore, here the electoral body may consist of a very large portion of the community. Thus, in English parishes, all rate-payers are qualified to vote, and to elect parish officers.

CXI.

But who will say that the affairs, home and foreign, of a great nation, are so simple that any one is competent to form an opinion upon them, and to elect a deputy to maintain that opinion?

CXII.

In all countries, without exception, the mass of the people have no deliberate, no independent judgment about such affairs; for they are too busy with their hands to work much with their heads.

CXIII.

Therefore, in no country, at least in no great country, having complicated relations, are the mass of the people qualified by knowledge to choose Legislators. You may educate as much as you can; but all your education will not exempt the people from the necessity of constant toil, and give them leisure to think.

CXIV.

There is, however, an expedient, by means of which a very large number, perhaps the greater number, may have part in a Parliamentary election. Though the mass be not qualified to form a serious opinion on state affairs, yet they may know in general who are the ablest and best men in their neighbourhood, who are the most active in parochial matters, who are the best guardians of the poor, the most efficient members of municipalities or Boards of Health, the most stirring county gentlemen. These are the men whom the people would naturally elect as delegates, and these delegates might choose the members of the legislature. This is the system of indirect election, which is valuable by allowing us to extend the primary franchise as widely as possible.

CXV.

Another advantage of this system is, that it enables us to extend the area of electoral districts so as to obviate local influences. The delegates, being comparatively few, may be collected from a large district, and may all meet at one place, there to elect not one but several representatives, after a discussion in common.

CXVI.

A third advantage of indirect election is, that the delegates, like the jury, not being known beforehand, "the eye of the tempter cannot see them, nor the hand of the powerful reach," provided they meet immediately after their nomination.

CXVII.

The President of the United States, and also the Senate, are chosen by indirect election, and these are triumphant instances. "The House of Representatives is composed for the most part of ordinary, nay vulgar men; but all remarkable talents find a place in the

Senate."[1] The President is chosen by electors nominated for that purpose alone; the Senators by the local legislature of each State.

CXVIII.

Upon the whole it appears that the opinion of Machiavelli and of Montesquieu, that the people (meaning the mass), is excellently fitted for the business of election, must be greatly modified. They are suited to elections for local purposes, not for State affairs; still less for high special appointments in Law, Physic, the Church, or the Army. If they participate at all in these, it should be only by indirect election.

CXIX.

In opposition to these views we are referred to the excellent selections of Consuls and others made by the Roman and the Athenian people.

CXX.

But the Roman Republic was very far from

---

[1] De Tocqueville.

a pure Democracy. The Consuls, Prætors, Censors, all *Curule* magistrates in short, were elected by the *Comitia Centuriata*, where the rich prevailed over the poor, the few over the many. It appears from Machiavelli himself that the Senate had great influence in the popular elections; for he tells us, that when afraid that the people would choose an obnoxious Plebeian, it always took care to bring forward either a very remarkable or a very ignoble man, to rally the mass by respect in the one case, to disgust them with Plebeians in the other.

CXXI.

As to the good selections made by the Athenian Democracy, that is a very questionable point. If there were many good, there were also many bad, and especially too many changes. We cannot forget that the policy of the State was directed for a time by the unworthy Cleon; that Chares and Lysicles, who lost the battle of Chæronea, had been preferred to Phocion; that the Sicilian expedition failed in great part from the incapacity of the commanders, such as Nicias; that a disaster having occurred during the absence of Alcibiades from his fleet, he instantly lost the popular favour and his command, a change which led to the ruin of Athens.

CXXII.

In a mixed government, such as that of Rome and of Great Britain, where an acknowledged and real Aristocracy prevails, that body is respected, and its members are likely to be chosen by the people for any office; and the more so, because an undoubted superiority gives rise to no jealousy. But where there is no real and acknowledged Aristocracy, it does not follow that intellectual superiority will be looked to in an election; for where all are proclaimed equal, the people become jealous of all superiority. This distinction is of great moment.

CXXIII.

The excellent results of Election, when properly organized, that is, when the electors are well-informed and sufficiently numerous, are remarkably shown in the long succession of eminent men who filled the office of Consul at Rome, of Doge at Venice and Genoa, and who continue to occupy the Papal chair. The Popes, it must be allowed, have been no common men. At Florence the chief magistrate, the *Gonfaloniere della justizia*, was chosen by popular suffrage. "This institution," says Roscoe, "had in the time of Lorenzo de' Medici, subsisted for nearly two hundred years, during which the office of Gonfaloniere had been filled by a regular succession of twelve hundred citizens, who had preserved the dignity and independence of the republic, and secured the exercise of their rights."[1] By this it appears that the office was held but for two months. The suffrage, though popular, was far from universal and equal; for the citizens voted by trades, and the *maggiori arti*, or greater trades, were seven, the *minori arti*, or lesser, were fourteen; though there were far more than twice as many individuals in the latter than in the former. "Even when democracy ran highest at Florence, it seems never to have been contemplated that all the influence of the rich and enlightened should

---

[1] *Life of Lorenzo*, Chap. VI.

be merged in an equal and universal suffrage. The utmost demanded was the formation of new corporate trades, which might balance the power of the higher."[1] Thus the principle of election was the same as at Rome in the *Comitia*, where the people voted not by head, but by tribe, or by century. By this expedient, suffrage may be universal, but not equal; all classes, even the poorest, may have some power, but not all power. What political wisdom in the old constitution of Rome!

CXXIV.

Excellent though election be, yet there are cases where it is not applicable.

(*a.*) *First*, It is not applicable where the prize is excessive; for in such a case the excitement would be too great, riot and conflict would be inevitable. These evils may be so serious as quite to outweigh the great advantages of election. Monarchy or Kingship is such a prize, it is too great to be contested. Hereditary descent, though a blind and appa-

---

[1] See the Author's *Political Discourses*, Dis. II., Chap. IV.

rently even an absurd ground of preference, is here far better than election, simply because it admits of no dispute. But hereditary monarchy is a standing testimony to the violence and waywardness of human nature. It is an acknowledgement that in the most important of all earthly concerns we cannot trust to our reason; that we are such children that chance is better for us than choice. If the prize be very great we must diminish it by shortening the time. Thus, if the chief magistrate of a State be elective, he ought to hold office for a brief period, as the President of the United States, who is chosen for four years. In the ancient republics and in Florence the period was much shorter. In Rome it was a year, in Florence two months, and at Athens a day, for the President of the Prytanes changed daily.

(*b*.) *Secondly*, There are cases where nomination by an individual is preferable to election by many. Thus, when a parish is divided into districts with several churches, it is highly desirable for the sake of unity and harmony throughout, that the nomination of ministers to the district churches should be with the Rector rather than with any other individual or body of men. It is also desirable that the Rector and his churchwardens should work well together; so, by the present law, the Rector nominates one, the parishoners elect the other. Moreover, discord is so at variance with true religion, that it is above all things to be avoided in the appointment of clergymen to vacant benefices. But discord is almost inseparable from election where the prize is valuable, as it is in the present instance; for the Rector is a man of the greatest importance in his parish, and he has generally a competence if not affluence for life. Therefore here, nomination by an individual patron, with all its drawbacks, seems preferable to any mode of election that has yet been devised. The people generally are quite incompetent to elect a clergyman. The utmost that should be trusted to them is a veto on the nomination, as now in the Established Church of Scotland.[1] Divines should be the proper electors; but we fear that electoral assemblies of divines would often be scenes of much

---

[1] Had this Veto been granted six months sooner, there would have been no schism, no Free Church.

scandal, of unseemly contests between High and Low. The partiality of individuals cannot be so injurious to the Church as the dissentions and broils of its clerical members, broils liable to be renewed at every election to a vacant benefice.

(c.) *Thirdly*, There are cases where nomination combined with a fixed rule is best. Election and implicit obedience to the person elected are hardly compatible. But obedience is the very soul of an army; unhesitating, unreasoning obedience. Therefore here also election is not applicable. In National Guards, in Militia, or in Volunteers, where regular attendance is enforced with difficulty, and where, consequently, it becomes important to conciliate and interest the men, election of officers may be allowed, as it is in the National Guard of France, also in our Volunteers, though contrary to the spirit of military discipline. An army is essentially monarchical, and the most that can be done is to limit individual partiality by some fixed rule.

In the English Army, the first nomination is by the Crown, but afterwards promotion up to a certain rank depends upon the rule of purchase. There is little danger in this, because almost any man can be made fit to be an inferior officer; but in the Navy, where the post of Lieutenant and of Captain is far more important and responsible, there is no purchase. Above the rank of Post-Captain, however, promotion goes entirely by seniority, and here again without danger, for a naval officer is attached to no corps, and if incompetent need never be employed; while by the time he has reached the rank of Post-Captain his competence or incompetence must be pretty well known. By these remarks we do not pretend to prove that the good of the service has always been chiefly consulted; it has often been sacrificed to the patronage and influence of Government.

End of the Aphorisms on Elections.

CXXV.

Poverty, Weakness, Cowardice, results of Despotism. "By these efforts Stilicho painfully collected from the subjects of a great empire an army of thirty or forty thousand men, which in the days of Scipio and Camillus would have been instantly furnished by the free citizens of the territory of Rome."[1] A.D. 406, *reg. Honorio*.

CXXVI.

Helplessness, the result of Centralization and Despotism. "When France was invaded by Charles V., he enquired of a prisoner, how many *days* Paris might be distant from the frontier; 'Perhaps *twelve*, but they will be days of battle:' such was the gallant answer which checked the arrogance of that ambitious prince. The subjects of Honorius and those of Francis I. were animated by a very different spirit; and in less than two years the divided troops of the savages of the Baltic, whose numbers, were they fairly stated, would appear contemptible, advanced, without a combat, to the foot of the Pyrenæan mountains."[2] A.D. 407.

Again, "In the time of Cæsar, Soissons would have poured forth a body of fifty thousand horse; but the courage and numbers of the Gallic youth were long since exhausted."[3]

---

[1] Gibbon's *Decline and Fall*, Chap. XXX.
[2] *Id.* Chap. XXX.   [3] *Id.* Chap. XXXVIII.

CXXVII.

"Trust not in Princes." Stilicho, the great Stilicho, was put to death by Honorius; Ætius, the renowned Ætius, was assassinated by the hand of Valentinian III.; the Douglas was stabbed by James II. of Scotland in Stirling Castle; the Duke of Burgundy was treacherously murdered by the Dauphin on the bridge of Montereau.

CXXVIII.

King and King-maker quarrel invariably. Instances:—Vespasian and Antonius Primus;[1] Leo the Great, Emperor of the East, and Aspar (A.D. 457); the Earl of Gloucester and Prince Edward (1267); Henry the IV. of England and the Earl of Northumberland; Edward the IV. and the Earl of Warwick; Richard the III. and Buckingham; Henry the VII. and Lord Stanley; Louis Philippe

---

[1] Antonius Primus, who commanded in Illyria, took up the cause of Vespasian, then in Judea, marched to Rome and defeated Vetellius; but he was despoiled of all power and treated ungratefully, first by Mucianus, sent to Rome by Vespasian, and afterwards by Vespasian himself.

and Laffitte; may we not add Absalom and Ahithophel; Victor Emmanuel and Garibaldi?[1]

CXXIX.

"If he could make, can he not unmake?" That thought is wormwood. The king grows cold and suspicious. What, thinks the king-maker, cold to me who uplifted him! base ingratitude! I ought at least to be second in the kingdom. Fool that I was to raise such a fellow to a throne! But, is there now no remedy? "Dive thoughts down to my soul." Woe to the man who slights the Earl of Warwick!

CXXX.

Whether the right of Primogeniture, in the Crown as well as in private families, was not introduced, or at least greatly strengthened, by our barbaric ancestors in Europe; and whether both these customs, at first sight con-

---

[1] As a reward for putting down the rebellion of 1715, and replacing the Scottish crown securely on the head of George I., the Duke of Argyle was deprived of all his employments.

trary to reason, be not in reality agreeable to profound political wisdom?

CXXXI.

What was said by Solon of his own laws applies at least to them, that though not the best that could be conceived, supposing men to be wiser and better, yet they are admirably adapted to the condition of men, as generally found; and surely this is very great praise.

CXXXII.

Hereditary Monarchy, in spite of its apparent absurdity, is universally preferable to an elective; but, in simple and virtuous societies, an elective Presidency may be better than either.

CXXXIII.

Who can doubt that the Cantons of Switzerland are better as they are, than if they were so many monarchies? The same of the United States.

CXXXIV.

But who can doubt that England is better as a Monarchy?

CXXXV.

We must not, however, mend coarse cloth with fine. We cannot blend things that have no affinity. Oil will not combine with water: Neither will monarchical unite well with republican institutions.

CXXXVI.

A Monarchy surrounded with republican institutions! When I see this work well I will believe in the Centaur.

CXXXVII.

A Monarchy harmonizes with an aristocracy, an Aristocracy with the right of primogeniture; all this is of a piece. The stuff may not be the finest, but it will wear well; it will serve for many a stormy day!

CXXXVIII.

An elective President, a democratic Parliament, Equality among children, Division of landed property; all this too suits well; the warp and the woof agree. The web too is of a finer texture, the work more highly finished; but it will not do for all climates. Admirably adapted to certain favoured regions, it would be rent to pieces by the blasts of a ruder sky.[1]

CXXXIX.

Either of these systems is feasible, consistent, logical; but when we would blend the two, we are apt to make strange work.

CXL.

Still, silk and worsted, linen and cotton, are woven together; though the mixture wear unequally.

CXLI.

So, the democratical element may certainly

---

[1] So long as the United States of America had no neighbours and no wars, so long as they possessed a boundless extent of new territory as a resource for their increasing population, so long the Republic prospered. But less than three years of war between the North and the South have changed the free Republic into a real military despotism. The *Habeas Corpus Act* is now suspended throughout all the Northern States, any one may be imprisoned and kept in prison contrary to law, a conscription is enforced at the point of the bayonet.—(*January* 1864.)

be mixed with the monarchical in a certain proportion, as it is in the British Constitution, and the whole still hold together; if they be closely bound by aristocracy.

CXLII.

Aristocracy is the connecting link, being attached at one end to monarchy, at the other to democracy. Loosen that and the whole falls to pieces.

CXLIII.

Aristocracy being gone, the monarch and the democracy are left as two eager combatants who fly at each other and fight it out, because there is no one to separate them. Both may suffer dreadfully, but one will destroy the other. Thus fell Charles X., thus fell Louis Philippe.

CXLIV.

Conclusion. The right of Primogeniture, which maintains an Aristocracy, is therefore necessary in a Monarchy; but Equality is the law of Republics.

CXLV.

Does it not follow from the above, that in attempting a Republic the French were at least consistent; for equality is there the law, and property is much divided? But equality is not only the law, it is also the taste of the people. In France, royalty and royal distinctions may not be distasteful, but aristocracy is decidedly odious.

CXLVI.

The obstacles to a Republic in France are the common obstacles, popular licentiousness, particularly in the great cities, and military power. Peculiar circumstances, however, are in favour of it, the state of property, and the state of opinion. But one peculiar circumstance is against it, the national character, too excitable, too changeable, and, we may add, too fond of war.

CXLVII.

Amid these conflicting elements who can presume to predict with confidence the future of France? One thing however is certain, that both speculation and experience show the instability of a Constitutional Monarchy in modern France; while a Republic has some decided points in its favour. In 1848 it was thought that the Republic had at last a fair chance; but how long did it last? Little more than three years, until the *coup d'état* of December 1851, which established a military government slightly veiled under republican forms. Universal suffrage, the panacea of democrats, was now found the best support of despotism.

CXLVIII.

If France do ever settle down into a Republic, it must disband the Army, and trust to the National Guard.

CXLIX.

Armies may in the course of time be disbanded; but national sympathies and antipathies will not change. Therefore France seems radically unfit for a Constitutional Monarchy duly supported by an aristocracy, not radically unfit for a Republic; and, consequently, *in the long run*, the Republic is likely to prevail. But the race may be very long, and limited Monarchy may first be tried again and again.

CL.

The horrors of ancient warfare are not to be told. We have already given a specimen of the *clemency* of Cæsar in Gaul. Germanicus was another noted for his mildness towards the conquered enemy, *mansuetudine in hostes*;[1] but attend to his doings in Germany. "Cæsar (Germanicus), that the devastation may be the wider, divides the eager legions into four wedges: he lays waste an extent of fifty miles with fire and sword; no pity is shown to sex or age."[2] Again, "Germanicus, the better to be recognized, had taken off the covering from his head, and entreated them to press on the slaughter; no need of captives, the extermination alone of the nation should be the end of the war."[3]

Under the philosophic Emperor Marcus Antoninus, the Roman generals penetrated as far as Ctesiphon and Seleucia. "The sack

---

[1] Tacitus, *Ann.* Lib. II. Cap. 72.
[2] *Id.* Lib. I. Cap. 51.   [3] *Id.* Lib. II. Cap. 21.

and conflagration of Seleucia, with the massacre of three hundred thousand of the inhabitants, tarnished the glory of the Roman triumph."[1] And well it might! Seleucia too, a friendly Greek colony! "After a signal victory over the Franks and Allemanni, several of their princes were exposed by order of Constantine to the wild beasts in the amphitheatre of Treves, and the people seem to have enjoyed the spectacle, without discovering in such a treatment of royal captives any thing that was repugnant to the laws of nature or of humanity."[2] Yet the Romans were a civilized people! It must be allowed that we have somewhat improved since that time. How much of this improvement is owing to Christianity?[3]

---

[1] Gibbon's *Decline and Fall*, Chap. VIII.

[2] *Id.* Chap. XIV.

[3] But we must not be too proud of our superior humanity. Consider the cruelties exercised by the French in Algeria, where men, women, and children were stifled in caves. Remember also the barbarities of Spaniards towards the French in the Peninsular war; the atrocities of the late contest in Hungary (1848-9); of the present strife in Poland; and last, not least,

CLI.

Contrast between the tranquillity enjoyed under the dominion of Rome, while its power continued unbroken, and the calamities which accompanied its decline and fall. "Three hundred years of peace, enjoyed by the soft inhabitants of Asia, had abolished the exercise of arms, and removed the apprehension of danger."[1] What a pregnant sentence! Three

---

the shelling and burning of Kagosima and of Sonderbörg: "The Prussians have bombarded Sonderbörg (an open town) 48 hours without any previous intimation. Eighty towns-people, women and children, have been killed or wounded. Fifteen hundred shells have been thrown into the town, which is deserted."—*Telegram from Ulkebol, April* 4, 1864. This account has never been contradicted. Still, on the whole, we have made a decided moral progress. Never were schemes of benevolence so general as now, never were greater sacrifices submitted to for the good of others. In his reply to the First of the Oxford *Essays and Reviews*, Dr Goulburn denies that the Christian religion has improved the moral sentiments and actions of mankind! Does not the learned Doctor see that he here cuts away the ground from his own feet? that by raising Christianity in air he severs its connection with earth?

[1] Gibbon's *Decline and Fall*, Chap. x.

hundred years of peace! Imagine a peace in Europe from the accession of Elizabeth to the present day! So much for the advantage of the Roman sway. But mark the change. From the year 248 to 268 there were twenty years of calamity, during which, as Gibbon says, it is probable that *the half of the human race* in the Roman Empire was destroyed by war, pestilence, and famine.

CLII.

Woe to the people who neglect the use of arms! woe to those who never fear danger! "The soft inhabitants of Asia," like the soft inhabitants of modern Italy, slumbered in security, till the sleep of the one was broken by the tramp of the Goth, of the other by the German and the Frank. During two hundred and fifty years of Italian prosperity, real war was almost forgotten, till the eagles of Charles VIII. and the French cavalry sounded across the Alps.

CLIII.

That peace is a great blessing, who can

doubt? but if peace render men unfit for war, that blessing may turn into a curse.

CLIV.
God may spare the weak, but man will not.

CLV.
If all Englishmen were Quakers, what would become of England? It would soon be a province of France. But the great Volunteer movement of 1859 and succeeding years has shown that England is neither all Quaker nor all Peace Society.

CLVI.
How uninteresting, how dead must have seemed the life in Imperial Rome to those who had shared in the turmoil of the Republic! Some are said to have died of mere ennui. The interest created in public affairs is no small advantage of Liberty. How trivial are the pursuits of the rich in despotic countries! The best possible despotism must at least be supremely dull.

CLVII.

The manners and morals of Rome under the first emperors were most extraordinary. What more remarkable than the patience with which men met death by order of the Emperor? *patientia servilis*, says Tacitus, *tam segniter perientes*. Their fortitude seems almost stupid insensibility; a strange mixture of Stoicism or philosophic resignation with servility!

CLVIII.

If servility be contemptible, how hateful is the despotism that causes it! Mark the following picture: "But in the Senate, the greater the grief, the more abject the flattery. He whose son, or brother, or relation, or friend had been put to death, returned thanks to the gods, adorned his house with laurel, threw himself at the feet of the emperor, and wore out his right hand with kisses."[1] Such had become the descendants of Scipio and Cato!

CLIX.

The above is bad enough, but what follows

---

[1] Tacitus, *Ann.* Lib. xv. Cap. 73.

is even worse. "The most deadly result of those times was, that that the chief men of the Senate acted as the lowest spies, some openly, many secretly."[1]

CLX.

"The gods have conferred on thee supreme power."[2] Speech addressed to Tiberius. The doctrine of divine right was thus early promulgated.

CLXI.

"Not even women were free from danger. Since they could not be convicted of aiming at supreme power, their tears were made a ground of accusation; and an old woman, Vitia, the mother of Fufius Geminus, was slain, because she had wept for the death of her son."[3] What could tyranny more?

CLXII.

"Nor was this any injury to Serenus, whom public hatred made more safe."[4]

---

[1] Tacitus, *Ann.* Lib. VI. Cap. 7.
[2] *Id.* Lib. VI. Cap. 8. [3] *Id.* Lib. VI. Cap. 10.
[4] *Id.* Lib. IV. Cap. 36.

CLXIII.

On occasion of a pestilence at Rome, Tacitus observes: "The deaths of Equites and Senators, although promiscuous, were less bewailed, as if they had anticipated by ordinary mortality the savage cruelty of the prince."[1] What must be the state of society where even a pestilence ceases to be an evil!

CLXIV.

Again, "Tiberius, excited by the capital punishments, orders all the prisoners accused of conspiracy with Sejanus, to be slain."[2]

CLXV.

"He had cut off sympathy by the force of fear; and the more savage he grew the more was pity restrained."[3] This is the climax! So much for despotism.

CLXVI.

There is no more striking instance in history of the effect of absolute power on the charac-

---

[1] Tacitus, *Ann.* Lib. XVI. Cap. 13.
[2] *Id.* Lib. VI. 19.   [3] *Id. id.*

ter, than that of Tiberius. Tiberius was not born to empire, he was fifty-five years old when he came into power, an age when former habits may well be supposed strong, and his previous life, we are told, had been good. Yet what a wretch he became! The restraint of his family, as long as it lasted, was of some use to him; but when Germanicus, his nephew, was dead, and Drusus, his son, and lastly, Livia, his mother, his excesses knew no bounds. Such is the consequence of the absence of *restraint*. "Tiberius," said Arrantius, "was violently shaken and changed by despotic power."[1]

CLXVII.

The excesses of Nero are less remarkable; for Nero was but a boy of seventeen when he became emperor.

CLXVIII.

Public opinion had some influence even on Nero; for he recalled his wife Octavia in consequence.

---

[1] Tacitus, *Ann.* Lib. VI. Cap. 48.

CLXIX.

The Senate condemned Antistius to death for songs injurious to the prince (Nero). On this Tacitus observes: "Some, lest they should seem to have exposed the prince to ill will; the greater part, safe in numbers."[1] This too was a case where Nero had written to the Senate to say, that they might acquit if they pleased. Mark the irresponsibility arising from numbers. Hence a large judicial tribunal is most improper, especially in political causes.

Who condemned Strafford? The Parliament by bill of attainder. Who condemned Charles I.? The Commons. Who condemned Louis XVI.? The Convention. Who condemned Ney? The Chamber of Peers. When secrecy is added to numbers, as in the French Chamber of Peers, all responsibility to the public is at an end.

CLXX.

Note the generous movement of the people to prevent the execution of all the slaves of

---

[1] Tacitus, *Ann.* Lib. XIV. Cap. 49.

Pedanius on account of the murder of their master by one of them.[1] This is quite agreeable to the nature of the multitude. It appears, however, that in spite of them the sentence of death was put in execution against all the slaves.

CLXXI.

Pedanius was prefect of the city. "Whom," says Tacitus, "shall the number of his slaves defend, if four hundred could not protect Pedanius Secundus?"[2]

CLXXII.

The above instances are drawn from the annals of a civilized people. What then should we expect in barbarous nations? To learn in what excesses a barbarous despot may indulge, read Captain Speke's account of Mtesa, king of Uganda. There a trifling breach of court etiquette is punished with death. "Nearly every day since I changed my residence, incredible as it may appear to

---

[1] Tacitus, *Ann.* Lib. XIV. Cap. 42, 45.
[2] *Id.* Cap. 43.

be, I have seen one, two, or three of the wretched palace women, led away to execution."[1] One woman, having presumed to offer a fruit to his majesty, was saved from instant death by the intervention of Captain Speke.

CLXXIII.

It is commonly said that the ancients were tolerant. Their religion was comprehensive, it embraced many deities, but it was not tolerant towards those who denied the gods of the country. The philosophic Tacitus thought the Christians worthy of death, merely on account of their religious belief; "*sontes et novissima exempla meritos*,"[2] though he allows that they excited pity because they were sacrificed to please a tyrant.

CLXXIV.

Under Tiberius "measures were taken for the expulsion of Egyptian and Jewish rites; and a decree of the Senate was passed, that

---

[1] *Journal of the Discovery of the Source of the Nile*, Ch. XII., p. 358.

[2] Tacitus, *Ann.* Lib. xv. Cap. 44.

four thousand freedmen infected with that superstition, of suitable age, should be transported to the island of Sardinia, to put down the robbers; if they should perish from the unhealthiness of the climate, it were little matter: the rest should leave Italy, unless before a certain day they had put away their profane rites."[1] At Athens, a price was put on the head of Diagoras as being an atheist, and Protagoras was banished on the same account. So much for toleration among the ancients.

CLXXV.

"The lust of rule," says Tacitus, "the strongest of all passions."[2] "In him, Pharasmanes, desire of supreme power was stronger than brother and daughter."[3] He, king of part of Armenia, put to death his own son, Rhadamistus.[4] So did Herod, king of Judea; so did Constantine; so Philip II. of Spain; so Czar Peter. It is worthy of note that three of these son-killers were styled *the Great.*

---

[1] Tacitus, *Ann.* Lib. II. Cap. 85.
[2] *Id.* Lib. XV. Cap. 53.   [3] *Id.* Lib. XII. Cap. 47.
[4] *Id.* Lib. XIII. Cap. 37.

CLXXVI.

How interesting is contemporary history to the readers of a later age! Small facts are related, in themselves perhaps of no great consequence, but which serve to show the genius of the times, or of an individual. Read the account of the embassy of Philo, the Jew, to Rome, and of his interview with Caligula. What a lively picture of the uneasy tyrant, who could not rest for a moment, but all the while kept running up and down his great reception room! Nero, we are told, was at table when the news was brought to him of the revolt of the legions. He rose instantly, and by his sudden movement overturned a lustre of enormous value. Who does not like to know that fact? Tacitus introduces Lepida, the mother of Messalina, exhorting her daughter to make away with herself! And the reflection of the historian thereupon is as remarkable. "But nothing honourable could enter a mind corrupted by lasciviousness."[1] "The custom was that the children of the prince should eat sitting, along with other

---

[1] Tacitus, *Ann.* Lib. XI. Cap. 37.

nobles of the same age, in the sight of their relations, at a separate and more frugal table."[1] *Sitting* not *reclining*. It was while at such a table that Britannicus, a boy of fourteen, was poisoned by Nero.

CLXXVII.

The above are a few specimens of the despotism of the Cæsars. But, according to Alexis de Tocqueville, modern democracy may bring it back again. Surely then he would resist Democracy. By no means. It is the predestined, the *necessary* future of the world. How comfortable!

CLXXVIII.

Tacitus, Machiavelli, Montesquieu, all are strongly in favour of the government of the three powers, which we call King, Lords, and Commons. This, it must be allowed, is some authority.

CLXXIX.

Who does not see the advantage of a medi-

---

[1] Tacitus, *Ann.* Lib. XIII. Cap. 16.

ator? Two persons, two bodies, two powers may fight as long as one survives; but when a third comes in, an agreement is made.

CLXXX.

Thus the pride of either is saved, for he yields not to his antagonist, but to a third party.

CLXXXI.

And the third will naturally side with the weaker, partly out of compassion, partly out of policy. Thus all three retain their rights.

CLXXXII.

This seems very simple; but the three powers are not always found.

CLXXXIII.

The more the pity; but where they are found, there let us preserve them.

CLXXXIV.

Pure Monarchy or despotism, and pure Democracy are the two extremes; but between these are many varieties of mixed government.

CLXXXV.

It is said that extremes meet. Agreeably to this axiom, there is more resemblance between pure Monarchy and pure Democracy than one might at first suppose.

CLXXXVI.

In the first place, both are founded on the principle of unity: in the one case, the will of the monarch; in the other, that of the majority of the people is supposed to be unquestioned and unquestionable. No individual, no body, no class must attempt for a moment to resist the monarchical or the popular will.

CLXXXVII.

This one principle leads to numerous consequences. If individuals, if corporate or other bodies, if classes of men were powerful, they might resist the will of the sovereign, whether monarch or people. Therefore the level of equality must be passed over individuals, all influential classes must be broken, all powerful corporations must be suppressed. This policy is common to despotism and democracy; to Persia and revolutionary France.

CLXXXVIII.

If the policy of the two be the same, then the one ought to facilitate the other. Thinking to work only for self, it must work for its rival also.

CLXXXIX.

True; but very many things are necessary to found a durable Democracy; whereas Despotism is easily raised. The one is like an exotic which must be carefully nursed; the other an indigenous plant which thrives without any care.

CXC.

Therefore Democracy is a better pioneer for Despotism, than Despotism for Democracy.

CXCI.

The revolutionary frenzy which overthrew the throne, laid low the clergy and the nobility, abolished the corporations, and effaced the Departments of France, certainly paved the way for the despotism of the Empire; and those who introduced equality into kingly Prussia, though they undermined the throne, did not thereby create a self-governing Democracy.

CXCII.

Such is the present state of great part of Europe. Thrones are shaken and insecure; but the people is unfit to govern.

CXCIII.

In a pure Monarchy, all power is derived from the monarch, and all public functionaries hold their places at his pleasure, and are responsible to him; while, in a pure Democracy, every one in place is answerable to the people. The master is different, but the dependence is alike. There is but one Autocrat, or one with many heads. No one else, no other individual or body, presumes to be self-dependent.

CXCIV.

Hence the result of both systems is not unlike, a tendency to court the ruling power, to conceal private opinion, to act a part, to fawn, to flatter. Those who are above such arts, that is the most virtuous, must keep aloof.

CXCV.

Pure Monarchy or Despotism naturally tends to tyranny, because the monarch has no effectual opponent. Every one, were he unopposed, would become a tyrant. But bodies of men have the same passions as individuals, and less responsibility. Why then should they not tyrannize over the dissentients, who are not worthy to be called opponents? If they reduce them to silence, is not this alone tyranny?

CXCVI.

Thus, in a pure and real Democracy, the majority is apt to oppress the minority. Strong in numbers, fortified by sympathy, conscious of resistless power, and removed from all responsibility, the many becomes a Tyrant, and the few their victims.

CXCVII.

This in a real Democracy. But how often

does a minority rule instead of the majority, and exercise a frightful tyranny in its name! Were the atrocities of the Reign of Terror the atrocities of the majority of Frenchmen, as they were said to be? or were they not in reality the acts of a very few? Did the Provisional Government of France in 1848 really represent the opinions and wishes of the nation, or merely the crude theories of Louis Blanc, and the passions of Ledru Rollin and his revolutionary associates? Of all despotisms none is so dangerous as the rule of a few in the name of the many.

CXCVIII.

The difficulty of founding a real Democracy is chiefly seen by this, that most attempts at it end, nay almost commence with the unlimited power of a few. The people is a cumbrous, unconnected, unserviceable body, and easily submits to be ruled by those who profess themselves friends.

CXCIX.

Does not this easy transformation of Democracy into Despotism show a marvellous analogy between them?

CC.

Some acute reasoners, deep thinkers, political rationalists in short, have advocated pure Democracy, others pure Monarchy; but those who unite experience and knowledge of men with ratiocination are generally in favour of mixed government.

CCI.

Hobbes was for absolute Monarchy, Harrington for pure Democracy, and they wrote *bonâ fide*. Bentham also was a sincere democrat. Plato drew up a plan of a model *Republic*, Sir Thomas More wrote his *Utopia*, Hume his *Idea of a perfect Commonwealth*, and Sièyes his *Constitution;* intellectual curiosities rather than serious schemes. All these, except More, were mere students, men of the closet. But Aristotle, whose experience of government was immense, Tacitus, Machiavelli, Montesquieu, Sydney, Burke, and Brougham, all well acquainted with men as well as with books, are loud in praises of mixed government.

CCII.

Montesquieu, it is well known, was a great admirer of the British Constitution. What he says of Harrington may be applied to Bentham also: that he built Chalcedon with the shore of Byzantium before his eyes.

CCIII.

According to Bentham, the Spanish Constitution of 1812 was far superior to the British.

CCIV.

Love of uniformity, of simplicity, of regularity, of consistency, may create an admiration of pure Monarchy or of pure Democracy; but these are idols of the human mind, idols of the race of man, which dazzle and blind us to truth.

CCV.

The genius of Bentham was, like that of Sièyes, systematic throughout. They would have ordered the world as a captain his men.

CCVI.

Nothing escapes the regulating mania of Bentham, from the tactics of a legislative assembly down to the size, form, and peculiar contrivances of a ballot-box. If mechanical means could secure secrecy, his plan would be perfect.

CCVII.

Harrington, though a sincere democrat, thought that the people, even a popular assembly of representatives, were totally unfit for deliberation. According to him, a smaller body, the senate, was to debate, the popular assembly only to adopt or reject without discussion.[1] On this model was formed the French Constitution of the year VIII. The *Tribunat* spake, the Legislative body was dumb, and voted.

CCVIII.

Strange that the scheme of a sincere demo-

---

[1] See Harrington's *Political Aphorisms*, Chap. v. Aph. 28.

crat should have found favour with one who aimed at an Imperial Crown!

CCIX.

Harrington asserts you might as easily find out when and where the soul of a man was in the body of a beast, as when and where the liberty essential to Democracy was in any other form than that of a senate and a popular assembly, with powers as above.[1] But who now thinks of such a scheme? Alas for dogmatism! Certainly scepticism is more becoming than dogmatism, more suitable to our ignorance; but unfortunately the two are often united in the same man.

CCX.

According to Harrington the senate should not exceed three hundred, nor the national assembly one thousand. These, as well as all elective bodies, are to be renewed by a third

---

[1] Harrington's *Political Aphorisms*, last Chap., Aph. 106.

annually. This is an essential part of his system, and one now extensively adopted. It is the law of England with respect to local Boards of Health, and municipal bodies generally, and seems a very wise regulation.

CCXI.

When two bodies are united mechanically, the qualities of the compound are a mixture of the qualities of the component parts; but when two substances are combined chemically, the qualities of the elements are lost and new properties appear.

CCXII.

Now, mixed government, which results from the union of the simple forms, seems, in some respects, more allied to a chemical than to a mechanical union; for though all the qualities of the elements do not disappear, yet new ones are brought to light.

CCXIII.

The quality which peculiarly belongs to mixed government, and neither to pure Democracy nor to pure Monarchy, is INDEPENDENCE.

CCXIV.

Under mixed government alone are found individuals, or bodies, or classes of men, who dare to stand alone, overawed neither by the frowns of a despot nor the cries and threats of the populace.

CCXV.

The existence of independent powers is of the very essence of mixed government. In a limited or mixed monarchy the King is irresponsible and constitutionally independent; the Nobles also are independent, and so sometimes are the Clergy, in their respective legislative assemblies. The Nobles likewise form the highest Court of Justice in the kingdom, and in that case also depend on no one. Under the feudal monarchies, the Nobles, individually, enjoyed extensive and independent powers.

CCXVI.

The tendency of such a system to encourage

independence of thought and character is self-evident. In a pure democracy, as well as in a pure monarchy, independence is suppressed by an omnipotent will.

CCXVII.

Whether the independence of character, for which Englishmen are so remarkable, be not mainly owing to the nature of their government?

CCXVIII.

Where there is independence, there will often be want of harmony, rivalry, contest. Therefore, in a mixed government there is always a struggle, and hence always a change going on, slowly perhaps, but certainly.

CCXIX.

But this struggle may be so moderated as to produce only a wholesome activity, not a feverish excitement and violence.

CCXX.

In a pure monarchy, on the contrary, there is no struggle, no political movement of any kind; and in a pure democracy there is no serious conflict of principles, only disputes about the details of administration.

CCXXI.

But these disputes about details may be carried on with as much vehemence as the more serious contests of mixed government.

CCXXII.

It is really edifying to see how Democracy and Despotism play into each other's hands.

CCXXIII.

Is the Nobility, the landed Aristocracy, the beneficed Clergy, to be smitten to the ground? Agreed. Is the right of Primogeniture to be abolished, land subdivided, the property of the Church to be confiscated for secular purposes? Again agreed. Are the Clergy, instead of lands and tithes of their own, to be paid by the State? and the Church to become the humble servant of the secular power? Content. Is an unpaid magistracy of landed gentry to be superseded by stipendiary justices? By all means. Is voluntary enlistment to be replaced by the conscription? Assuredly. Are local bodies to be cramped in their action, and made more and more dependent on the Central Government? It is well. Is the Central Power, in short, to grow at the expense of all individuals, associations, corporations, or classes of men? That is our common object. The Spirit of modern Democracy and of pure Monarchy agree in so many points, that it is hard to say wherein they differ.

CCXXIV.

Napoleon had no occasion to remodel France to suit Imperial Despotism; the *Assemblée Constituante*, the *Assemblée Legislative*, and the *Convention Nationale*, had saved him the trouble. They had done all he could wish.

CCXXV.

So had the Long Parliament worked for Cromwell. The Presbyterians upset the Church, the Independents the Throne, and both did away with the Lords; afterwards Cromwell and his army had it all their own way.

CCXXVI.

Upon the whole, may we not conclude that mixed government, such as a limited Monarchy, though it seems a mean between pure democracy and pure monarchy, differs in reality from both more than either of these differs from the other?

OF THE FEDERAL SYSTEM.

CCXXVII.

The FEDERAL SYSTEM, which took its origin among the Republics of antiquity, has in modern times undergone some remarkable developments and modifications.

CCXXVIII.

But what is the Federal System? What are its characteristics?

CCXXIX.

The Federal System is founded on the union of the Central with the Local System, giving, however, the preponderance to the latter. This is the prevailing idea, from which all federal institutions flow.

CCXXX.

Agreeably to this fundamental idea, a Federation supposes an union of States not of Provinces, of States sovereign and independent, not of Provinces subordinate.

CCXXXI.

But there can be no union without a bond, and no bond without mutual concession. Therefore, each of these Sovereign States must give up a portion of its sovereignty to a Central Power for the sake of combination.

CCXXXII.

What is given up to the Central Power must, of course, be defined as accurately as possible. In every thing not expressly excepted, the States retain their sovereignty. On the contrary, when local privileges are granted to provinces by the central power as sovereign, whatsoever is not expressly conceded to the province is retained by the central authority.

CCXXXIII.

These are the essentials of the Federal

System: States sovereign with undefined powers; Central government sovereign only in a limited and definite sphere.

CCXXXIV.

The States united by the Federal bond may be either Republics or Monarchies. There is nothing in the nature of Federation to exclude one more than the other.

CCXXXV.

Among the ancients we find examples only of Federal Republics on a small scale; but in more recent times we have instances of Confederate Republics on a vast scale, and even of Confederate Monarchies.

CCXXXVI.

In the United States we see the signal triumph of the Federal System. About thirty Republics, some of them as extensive as England, enjoy, under this system, free local government, along with national union and power,—harmony at home, and force abroad.[1]

---

[1] This was written before the late most unhappy

CCXXXVII.

Before the rise of this great Federation, Europe had seen and admired the Hanseatic League, the Federal Republics of Holland and Switzerland. She had witnessed the same principles applied to monarchies also.

CCXXXVIII.

The union of Colmar in 1397 was an union of three independent kingdoms, Sweden, Denmark, and Norway, under a central government, in the person of Queen Margaret, the Semiramis of the North, with a common diet, composed of the states of the three kingdoms, assembled at Helmstadt.

CCXXXIX.

The old German Confederation, before the French Revolution, was a Federal union of Monarchies, lay and ecclesiastical, some small, some great, together with some free towns. This seems to be the only attempt on record

---

separation between the North and the South, but the success of the system for upwards of 70 years cannot be disputed.

to unite Monarchies and Republics by a Federal bond. This system still, in part, exists, for Hamburg, Frankfort, and other free towns are in league with the kingdoms and duchies of Germany.

CCXL.

The central power of Germany, as fixed by the Congress of Vienna after the fall of Napoleon, consists of a Diet, composed of the representatives of sovereign Princes, sixteen in number, sitting at Frankfort, without any popular assembly. Seven of the smallest States have only one representation in common.

CCXLI.

What a laborious effort was made in 1848-9 to reform this compact, and how fruitless!

CCXLII.

Two leading ideas seem to have been present to the Reformers of Germany, particularly to the members of the Frankfort Parliament of 1848-9, namely, consolidation, and extension of popular power. They wished to raise a German Empire, and to establish Democracy beside it. Singular and incongruous union!

CCXLIII.

Observe that the extreme Democrats were also extreme in their views of Consolidation. They would have sacrificed the Independence of all the smaller states for the sake of Unity; they would have abolished the Federal system entirely. They laboured, as they thought, for an uniform Democracy, but, in reality, for an uniform Despotism. Fools to suppose that an Emperor with the forces of all Germany at his disposal would care much for a democratical assembly! Here we see again how Democracy works for Despotism.

CCXLIV.

The great powers of Germany, Austria, and Prussia, do not respect even the Diet. They have just been outvoted by eleven to five on the Sleswig-Holstein question, and yet they utterly disregard the decision. The Austrian Minister, Count Rechberg, said very cooly that Austria and Prussia could not allow themselves to be outvoted in the Diet! *January* 1864.

CCXLV.

The notion of a German Empire, along with a real Democracy, was absurd and contradictory, and therefore in practice impossible; but one *or* the other was, at least, not incongruous, though, in the actual state of Germany either was unattainable.

CCXLVI.

How could a people unused to any self-government be prepared for a Democracy? How were the troops to be managed? Were *they* all democrats? On the other hand, so long as Austria and Prussia were existent each in his strength, how could there be one Emperor and one Empire? Had Austria fallen in her contests with Italy and Hungary, then the King of Prussia might have become Emperor of Germany; but so long as there were two great powers, neither could be supreme. The politicians of Frankfort thought to exclude Austria from Germany! Good easy men!

CCXLVII.

Had Austria fallen, and Prussia risen on her ruins, she would have consolidated Germany, she would have created an Empire; but would Democracy, would liberty have gained? They who think so must have more trust in princes than I. Do monarchs generally become more yielding when they become more powerful?

CCXLVIII.

Prussia had already made great strides to Empire, she had spread her forces from the Baltic to the Black Forest, while she amused and cajoled the Democracy with a mimic parliament at Erfurt: when lo! the sun of Austria emerged from eclipse, and the star of Prussia grew pale. The phantom of an Emperor struggled for a moment with the returning light, made many contortions and threatening gestures, seemed bigger as it waxed thinner, and finally vanished in mist with a piercing cry.

CCXLIX.

If proof were before wanting, this recent

history would prove that the Federal System alone is suited to Germany.

CCL.

The connection now existing between Sweden and Norway is another instance of the Federal System applied to Monarchical States; for each of these States considers itself sovereign and independent, and they are united under one King.

CCLI.

The first Article of the Norwegian Constitution of November 4, 1814 is as follows: "The Kingdom of Norway is a free State, indivisible and inalienable, united to Sweden under the same King."

CCLII.

Moreover, provision is made for the choice of a Regency, or of a new Dynasty on the failure of the old; and in this choice Norway and Sweden have equal parts; a proof of the constitutional equality of the two kingdoms.

CCLIII.

Besides, various Articles of the Constitution show that the Legislature of Norway claims to interfere in affairs *external* as well as *internal*, and consequently it is not a merely local and a subordinate legislature.

CCLIV.

Therefore, Sweden and Norway together form a Federal Monarchy; though there be no common legislature.

CCLV.

A common legislature, diet, or congress, is then no essential part of the Federal Sytem.

CCLVI.

A common constitutional link, no doubt, there must be; but "the golden link of the crown" may suffice.

CCLVII.

Observe that most of the important questions which, under a Federal Republic, appertain to a common legislature or congress, belong, under a monarchy, to the king alone.

CCLVIII.

Such are the questions of peace and war; diplomatic relations; treaties with foreign powers, political or commercial; high judicial appointments. These are all within the province of the American Congress, either of both houses or of the Senate alone,[1] along with the President; but under a monarchy they are prerogatives of royalty.

CCLIX.

There is therefore less occasion for a common legislature in a Federal Monarchy than in a Federal Republic.

CCLX.

Two questions however there are, of great importance, requiring a decision in common, which the king under a constitutional system cannot settle alone. These are the question of succession to the throne or of a regency;

---

[1] The President, along with a majority of two-thirds of the Senate, makes treaties and confers diplomatic and high judicial appointments; but war or peace can be declared only by both houses of Congress and the President.

and questions of tariff, either in trade with foreign nations, or between the different States of the Federation.

CCLXI.

The first difficulty has thus been provided for by the Norwegian Constitution. Should the two Diets of Sweden and Norway disagree in their choice of a King or of a Regent, a Committee is chosen consisting of thirty-six members, eighteen from each Diet, who meet at Carlstadt, a frontier town of Sweden, to decide the question. But, in order to avoid the possibility of equality, one member is excluded by *lot* before the votes are given. Thus, supposing the Swedes unanimous in their choice, as well as the Norwegians in theirs, it is clear that according as the lot falls on a Swede or a Norwegian, the Norwegian or the Swedish candidate will prevail.

CCLXII.

How great must be that difficulty which *lot* alone can decide; when a kingdom too is at stake! lot, the last resource of equal competitors, or of helpless indecision!

CCLXIII.

This is the great stumbling-block of Federal Monarchy. Who can decide when equals disagree? Questions of trade may be amicably settled, they admit of compromise; but the succession to the throne is a more serious affair, and in general admits of no compromise.

CCLXIV.

Great Britain and Ireland, with their mutual relations from the year 1782, the era of the independence of the Irish Parliament, down to the Union, present another instance of the Federal System.

CCLXV.

No one, however, seems to have remarked that it was a real example of such a system. Nay, O'Connell and the Repealers who worked for its return, considered simple Repeal as quite different from Federation. They upheld the former, and argued against the latter, which, as they understood it, was not Federation at all, but quite a different scheme, to be explained presently.

CCLXVI.

What then were the mutual relations of Great Britain and Ireland during the brief but brilliant period above referred to?

CCLXVII.

By the declaration of Independence moved by Grattan, on the 16th of April 1782, and carried unanimously, and especially in the address to the king founded upon it, it was maintained that, "the kingdom of Ireland is a *distinct Kingdom*, with a Parliament of her own, the sole legislature thereof; that there is no body of men competent to make laws to bind the nation but the King, Lords, and Commons of Ireland; nor any Parliament which hath any authority or power of any sort whatever in this country, save only the Parliament of Ireland." Nothing can be more unqualified than this assertion of Sovereignty and Independence. At the same time it is asserted that "the Crown of Ireland is an *Imperial Crown*, inseparably connected with the Crown of Great Britain, on which connection the interests and happiness of both nations essentially depend." Here then we have Ireland and Great Britain each an Independent Kingdom, but united by a common link, the link of the Crown; just as Sweden and Norway; and therefore the system was truly Federal. As in the case of Sweden and Norway, there was no common legislature, but that, we have seen, is not essential.

CCLXVIII.

The two questions which we have mentioned as the grand difficulties of Federal Monarchy failed not to embarrass the relations of Great Britain and Ireland under their short Federal union. "Three years after the declaration of Independence, an attempt was made to settle the commercial relations between Great Britain and Ireland by treaty; but not all the talents of Pitt could bring it to a conclusion. In 1789 came on the Regency question; and here a direct collision took place between the two Parliaments: the British Parliament, under the direction of Pitt, gave the Regency to the Prince of Wales, but with a restricted prerogative; while the Irish Parliament endowed him with all the kingly powers."[1] The recovery of the king fortunately put an end to the dispute.

CCLXIX.

The Union between Great Britain and Ireland obviated these difficulties, and it probably contributed to the power and security of the Empire; but who can believe that with an Independent Parliament Ireland ever could have been reduced to the wretchedness which she has since experienced? The unexampled prosperity of Ireland during the brief period of her Independence speaks loudly against such a supposition.

CCLXX.

Ministers of State hate difficulties; Irish Independence was a difficulty; therefore it was to be got rid of at all costs.

CCLXXI.

Ireland, indeed, might be worse off; but

---

[1] See my *Proposal for a Restoration of the Irish Parliament*, p. 18. Dublin, 1845.

what of that, if Downing Street were less perplexed?

CCLXXII.

The agitation for the Repeal of the Union was perfectly natural; for material prosperity as well as national dignity had declined.

CCLXXIII.

Had the Union been even good for Ireland, yet the mode in which it was carried must have rendered it odious.

CCLXXIV.

Tell me which is morally worst? He who gives or he who receives a bribe? It is hard to say; but we all know which is the most despicable.

CCLXXV.

But which is most despicable, a poor man, or a rich, high-born, well educated man receiving a bribe? If the latter, then the Irish Peers, and Commons raised to the peerage, who voted the Union, for money or for rank, are the last in the scale of ignominy.

CCLXXVI.

The same cause which has proved fatal to almost every political movement in Ireland prevented also the Repeal of the Union, namely, want of unanimity, especially religious differences; for with all their engaging, all their good qualities, the Irish have ever been, individually and nationally, the most quarrelsome of mankind.

CCLXXVII.

The sincerity of the Repeal Chief may also be questioned. To him the agitation for Repeal was most lucrative, always a suspicious circumstance; and when nearest his object he shrunk back, apparently scared "at the sound himself had made."

CCLXXVIII.

People who cannot govern themselves are sure to be governed by others. Witness Ireland and Poland. The best excuse for the rule of England over Ireland, and of Russia over Poland, is the tried incompetence of the the two for political combination. In politics the greatest of faults is the want of concord. This alone can make, the want of it mars a nation.

CCLXXIX.

Austria and Hungary, before the revolution and civil war of 1848-9, afforded another instance of a Federal Monarchy; for each was an Independent and Sovereign State in all particulars not specified in the pacts of Union of 1463, 1491, and 1724, the last being the Pragmatic sanction. These particulars referred to the link between the two Kingdoms, the Crown, with all its prerogatives of war and peace, diplomacy, and treaties. Austria was a pure Monarchy, Hungary a limited Aristocratic Monarchy, and the Emperor of Austria was King of Hungary.

CCLXXX.

The great Hungarian movement of the years 1848-9 seems to have been partly national, partly aristocratic. So far as it went to establish the supremacy of the Magyars over the other races inhabiting Hungary, it was aristocratic; so far as it aimed at Independence with reference to Austria, it was national. This diversity of objects made the Hungarian cause less popular with the rest of Europe than otherwise it would have been. It was a complicated affair, and impartial men hardly knew what to wish. Inasmuch as the aim was complete independence and separation from Austria, the movement in its causes and object bore a great resemblance to the Irish rebellion of 1799; and the result hitherto has been the same, loss of Hungarian Independence and a more intimate union with Austria. As then in Ireland, so in Hungary, wild democratic ideas, stirred up in both cases by Revolutions in France, were united with national feelings; and if Ireland had her Wolf Tone, Hungary had her Kossuth. The most remarkable difference between the two movements consists in this, that whereas in Ireland it was the people who moved and the aristocracy who resisted; in Hungary, on the contrary, the aristocracy of the Magyars took the lead in the revolt. The Irish rebellion was a pure national movement, for it aimed at no supremacy of class; but it was foolish, for it had no chance of success: whereas the Hungarian revolt was of a mixed character, though by no means silly; for the Hungarians would have triumphed but for the interference of Russia.

CCLXXXI.

More recently, in 1860–1, another attempt has been made by Hungary to achieve her Independence. The movement seems to have been simplified and purified by time, its aristocratic tendency has disappeared, and it has become thoroughly national. Hungary will not send deputies to the Reichrath at Vienna; she upholds her Federal position, her independent Diet, and her Union with Austria by the Crown alone.

CCLXXXII.

It must be allowed, that the examples of Ireland and Hungary are not much in favour of Federal monarchy without a common legislature. The link of the Crown seems not enough to complete the system; a common or central legislature, meeting, perhaps, only occasionally, is desirable.

CCLXXXIII.

This common legislature would settle those questions which cannot be decided by one State alone of the Confederacy, nor yet by the king alone, particularly questions relating to foreign trade, or trade between the Confederate States, and those concerning the succession to the crown and the civil list. The attributes of this common legislature would be few but important.

CCLXXXIV.

The Federation of Germany differs from all others in this, that there are not only a number of Sovereign States, but also a number of Kings or Royal Dukes.

CCLXXXV.

So long as all power in each State was lodged in the king alone or royal duke, so long a common Diet at Frankfort composed of these princes alone, or their representatives, was in harmony with the political condition of the several members of the Confederacy. But when popular assemblies became a part of the

Constitution of one or more of the States, then there arose an incongruity between the Central Diet and the institutions of the Free States. If, indeed, the Diet of Frankfort were to limit its decisions to questions strictly within the prérogative of a Constitutional King, there would be no such incongruity; but, were it to go beyond these limits, then the rights of the free states would be violated. Nor can we doubt that an assembly of kings, with the power in their hands, would overstep those limits. At home they would be hampered by a popular assembly, but at Frankfort they would be quite at ease, and ready to assist each other against the common foe, popular encroachment. Therefore a central popular Chamber becomes a necessary check to the power of a Congress of Princes, necessary for the freedom of the several States, as well as for the settlement of questions, such as those above enumerated, which a Constitutional King, or many Constitutional Kings, have no right to decide.

CCLXXXVI.

Now, Austria, Prussia, Bavaria, Saxony,

Hanover, and Wurtemberg, and other States of the Confederacy, actually possess popular representative assemblies.

CCLXXXVII.

Therefore, what above all is wanted to improve the Federal System of Germany is a central popular Assembly at Frankfort.

CCLXXXVIII.

Considering the vast standing armies now kept on foot by Austria and Prussia, a popular assembly may be but a feeble check to kingly power; but it must be tried.

CCLXXXIX.

No doubt, if it resembles the Frankfort Parliament of 1848, it will not last long.

CCXC.

It must not, then, be a wild democratic Chamber, which would stir up a contest to end in its own ruin.

CCXCI.

How then shall it be chosen? I answer,

by indirect election; the advantages of which have been already shown.

CCXCII.

Let the Deputies be elected by the Legislative Assembly of each State of the Confederacy, as is the Senate of the United States of America, but in number proportioned to the population of each State, like the House of Representatives. Since the questions to be brought before them are not many, the assembly need not be numerous; and a few deputies thus chosen would be superior men. This would be the Lower Chamber of the Federal Diet.

CCXCIII.

The Upper Chamber, on the other hand, should consist, as the Diet at present, of the representatives of all the Sovereign Princes of Germany. Since the difference is so great between the size of the different States, we do not propose that each should have the same number of votes, as in the American Senate; but, at the same time, in order to preserve the Federal principle, the independence of each

State, it is necessary that the smaller should be amply represented, much more amply than their population would warrant. The Upper Chamber, like the American Senate, should be the especial guardian of State Independence.

CCXCIV.

Such then should be the two Chambers of the Federal Diet. But who should be the Head of Germany?

CCXCV.

In the first place, it is clear that the sovereign Princes of Germany are too numerous a body to form all together a central Executive, which requires unanimity, promptitude, and energy, qualities not often found in numbers.

CCXCVI.

Therefore, the central Executive must be composed of a smaller number selected from the whole body of sovereign heads.

CCXCVII.

Still the question remains; shall the Head of all Germany be one or more than one?

CCXCVIII.

That the Executive Government should be vested in one, is a maxim which has been adopted not only in all Monarchies, despotic, feudal, or constitutional, but even in some of the best regulated Republics; in Holland with its Statholder, Venice and Genoa with their Doges, and in the United States with their President. The practice of antiquity, no doubt, was different; as is that of Switzerland with its Federal Directory.

CCXCIX.

Where can unanimity, promptitude, energy, and responsibility be found in perfection if not in one? In all these particulars, essential to a good Executive, one is better than two, three, or many.

CCC.

In a plural Executive there will either be constant discord, or one in reality will rule the rest; but he will rule in the name of all, and thus his individual responsibility will be under cover.

CCCI.

For this reason a Triumvirate has been very agreeable to ambitious men. Till the power of Napoleon became fully established, two colleagues in the Consulate, two men of straw, were very convenient. The over-weening ambition of both Cæsar and Pompey was masked by their association with Crassus; as that of Octavius and Antony by Lepidus. The two French Consuls were easily set aside, like Lepidus, when they had served a turn.

CCCII.

Nothing is more dangerous to a State than discord in the Executive; but if One in reality rule, he had better rule in his own name. In the French Directory of five there was generally discord; in the Consulate unanimity, because one master mind ruled the other two. To judge by the Republican Constitution of 1848, the French had no wish again to try a plural Executive.

CCCIII.

We cannot therefore doubt that in general

the Executive power is best in the hands of one. But we may still inquire whether in Germany this be possible or advisable.

CCCIV.

Let us consider what is the actual political state of Germany. That great country contains six kingdoms and several minor principalities, with four free towns; and of the six kingdoms, two are far superior to the rest in territory and in power. Therefore, whatever form the Central or Federal Executive may assume, we may rest assured that the principal influence will remain with these two.

CCCV.

If the principal power will really reside with these two, why not openly give it to them, agreeably to the principles above laid down?

CCCVI.

Were there but one power in Germany very superior to all the rest, there could be no difficulty; but the existence of two complicates the question.

CCCVII.

These two kingdoms being both great, and rivals in power, there can be no peace so long as either is dissatisfied. Therefore there must be a compromise; neither alone must be supreme.

CCCVIII.

Consequently, there can be no Emperor of Germany. Formerly the Empire was hereditary in the House of Austria, but the rise of Prussia and her actual pretensions render such an Empire now impossible.

CCCIX.

But we have seen that in general the Executive power is best in the hands of One; and, in this instance, two powers of equal pretensions cannot be expected to work harmoniously together as heads of Germany.

CCCX.

If then both must have a share in the supreme power, while yet they cannot act together, what remains but to enjoy it separately, that is, by rotation?

CCCXI.

Such then is our conclusion. The Federal Executive of Germany should be vested in the Emperor of Austria and the King of Prussia alternately, either year by year, or for a period not exceeding four years for each.

CCCXII.

The principle of rotation, here recommended for Kingdoms forming part of a monarchical confederation, has long been applied in Switzerland to Cantons; for each of the three great Cantons, Bern, Lucerne, and Zurich, is alternately the governing or directing Canton of the Confederacy.

CCCXIII.

After three years of vain theories, wild schemes, and fruitless efforts at amendment, the German Diet, as constituted in 1815, again met at Frankfort (May 14, 1851). May the revived Diet reform itself to suit the wants of the age! I have suggested a plan of reform, a private individual can do no more.

CCCXIV.

The great Federal Republic of North America differs from all previous federations in this, that it has not only a common Legislature or Congress and a common Executive or President, but also a common Administration. In Switzerland, on the contrary, though there is a Federal Diet and a Federal Directory, yet the Directory has no subordinate officials for the execution of the decrees of the Diet, which are therefore entrusted to the local authorities. The Federal bond is consequently much more close in the American union, where the Central Government has its own civil functionaries, its own treasury, its own court of justice, and its own army. The American Confederacy is properly called the United States; that of Switzerland, States in union. The latter has hitherto been the character of the the German Confederation. The "Execution" now being carried on in Holstein is not effected by a Federal army, but by the forces of Austria, Prussia, Saxony, and Hanover acting in the name of the Federation. (*January, February* 1864.)

CCCXV.

A principal difficulty of the Federal System is the settlement of disputes between the different States, each sovereign and independent, and between the States and the Central power. The Federal Diet or Congress is itself hardly impartial, for if the dispute be between two States, each being represented in that body, they must vote in their own cause; and if the Diet itself be one of the parties, much less can its decisions be free from suspicion. Of all the institutions of the United States none is more highly approved of than the FEDERAL TRIBUNAL to which such questions appertain; none has more contributed to the maintenance of the Union. Such an institution might be found a great improvement in the future constitution of the Germanic Confederation.

Since the above was written, the differences between the North and South, in the want of an impartial arbiter, have led to the separation of the Union into two camps. There was no third party of sufficient weight by whom those differences might have been reconciled; and therefore recourse was had to the sword. May this suicidal contest soon terminate! Such is my wish rather than my expectation. One cannot forget that the Peloponnesian war between States similar in language, race, arts, and arms, as are the Americans, lasted twenty-seven years, and the great German war thirty years. In all probability the South will achieve its independence; so the sooner the North gives up its ambitious projects the better.

CCCXVI.

The Federal System is ill-suited to conquest, admirably adapted for defence. Higher praise cannot be bestowed.

CCCXVII.

The Federal System is ill-suited to conquest, on account of the diversity of opinions, of interests, of passions, which must exist among several sovereign States, all but independent of each other. So many different political bodies can hardly be brought to join unanimously and cordially in any thing so questionable, so hazardous, so burdensome, as a plan of foreign conquest.

CCCXVIII.

But when the Confederacy is attacked, the case is widely different. Palpable interest then tightens the bond of union, and the States act as one. For the time, they enjoy all the advantages of a central and vigorous government; while they do not entirely depend on it. Each State has in itself a centre of action; and may resist even after the defeat of the Federal power. The local spirit which prevails in the States rouses the people to extraordinary energy. The finest army then in Europe, that of the Duke of Burgundy, was scattered like chaff at Granson and at Morat by the despised peasants of Switzerland; and when Republican France had subdued Bern and the low country, the forest Cantons still kept up the unequal contest.

CCCXIX.

Here we may quote those remarkable words of Napoleon, addressed to the Swiss deputies who came to advocate the cause of an Unitarian Switzerland. "To be free at home, invincible, respected, is a condition sufficiently dignified. For such, the Federal System is best. It has less of that unity which dares, but it has more of that inertia which resists."

CCCXX.

In internal affairs the Federal System offers as many advantages as in foreign relations. It admirably combines the Central with the Local system; the unity and power of the one, with the liberty, variety, and life of the other. It links together order and freedom. It is applicable not only to small States, but to very extensive territories; not merely to Holland and Switzerland, but to the vast continent of North America. This last is its peculiar advantage. It is the only system of freedom by which great regions of the earth can form but one nation. Despotism indeed may unite all people and languages, but Freedom can combine them only under the Federal System. While the Russian eagle was flying undisturbed from the Baltic to the Straits of Behring, the stars and stripes of red bunting waved in the gale from the St Lawrence to the Gulph of Mexico.[1]

---

[1] By the royal Declaration or Patent of March 30,

CCCXXI.

Union has ever been the great want of Italy, from the fall of the Roman Empire in the West down to the present day. It was the consciousness of this want that induced Machiavelli to compose his *Principe*, to show how despotic power might be gained, and to desire the concentration of Italy even under a Borgia. *Union, union, union*, was his watchword, as that of Petrarch was *Peace, peace, peace:* and the latter can be secured only by the former. The distracted state of Italy in the time of Machiavelli moved a true lover of freedom to wish for despotism, and even to palliate enormities which might lead to union.

1863, Holstein and Lauenburg were made independent sovereign States in all respects except the golden link of the Crown connecting them with Denmark. This then was another instance in Europe of the Federal Monarchical System. But as thus Holstein was separated from Sleswig, Germany took umbrage and the Patent was repealed. What Austria and Prussia now profess to wish is the same system applied to Holstein and Sleswig united. (*February* 1864.)

Violence has since changed all this.

CCCXXII.

A wise head, the present Emperor of the French, proposed the Federal System for Italy; and apparently with good reason; for who could have supposed that so many sovereign independent States, long separated by local antipathies, would discard their rulers, give up their mutual jealousies, and unite under a common sovereign? This is the great wonder of our times, the astonishment and joy of liberal Europe! And yet an uniform centralized system, like that of France, is not suited to Italy; and none but a Mazzini would attempt it. What then remains? A system somewhat akin to the Federal, yet essentially different from it, alike in form more than in reality, free from the dangers, but partaking many of the advantages of the Federal System. This I would call

THE PROVINCIAL SYSTEM.

CCCXXIII.

The Provincial System supposes a Nation divided into Provinces, each with its own local institutions, not sovereign as in the Federal System, but dependent on the Central or Imperial Government, to which each Province sends representatives.

CCCXXIV.

The essential parts of this system are then separate Provincial institutions, and representation of each Province in the Central or General Assembly.

CCCXXV.

The essential difference between this and the Federal System is, that in the latter the States are Sovereign and independent, in the former not. Also, the Federal System, as we have seen, may exist without a common representative assembly, not so the Provincial.

CCCXXVI.

Since in the Provincial System the local legislatures are not sovereign bodies, their powers must be defined, and nothing belongs to them which is not expressly stated; while the central and imperial legislature being supreme, its powers are indefinite, and may be extended or contracted at pleasure. The contrary is the case in the Federal System.

CCCXXVII.
Thus the two systems, though they wear an air of resemblance, are in reality opposed.

CCCXXVIII.
A common representative assembly is not essential to the Federal System, because each State is sovereign; and what belongs to all, and is strictly defined, may be left to the one King; but were dependent Provinces not represented in an imperial legislature, they could have no political liberty, they would be at the mercy of the supreme ruler.

CCCXXIX.
It is evident that the union is much more close in the Provincial than in the Federal System; for in the former there is but one Sovereign, in the latter many.

CCCXXX.
The Provincial System was brought forward and proposed for Ireland by the Author of

these *Aphorisms* in the year 1845, when the Repeal agitation was at its height;[1] and four years afterwards the very same system was promulgated by Austria, as the Constitution of the Austrian Empire.[2] By this she did away with the Independence of Hungary, Croatia, and other states, and made them Provinces with local legislatures, and with a share in a common Legislature or Reichrath at Vienna.

CCCXXXI.

That Austria was in earnest in wishing to destroy the independence of the States there can be no doubt; that she then seriously meant to grant popular representative institutions may well be doubted. After a slumber of more than ten years, this Constitution has been revived. During more than ten years

---

[1] See *A Proposal for the Restoration of the Irish Parliament*, which, though advocating a system essentially different from Repeal, was thought worthy of being published along with the Prize Essays on the Repeal of the Union. Dublin, 1845.

[2] See the Austrian Constitution of March 1849, revived October 21, 1860.

the promise was neglected; will it be better kept now? In any case Hungary will have none of it.

CCCXXXII.

It must in fairness be allowed that at last Austria is acting up to her promises. At this time (February 1864) all the States composing the Austrian Empire have local popular assemblies, and all are represented in the common Legislature or *Reichrath* at Vienna, that is to say, all that will accept this Constitution; for Hungary and Venetia reject the boon. Hungary desires her ancient Federal union with Austria, an independent Parliament, and only the link of the Crown; while Venetia repels Austria altogether. Transylvania has just acceded. Even the small States, the Bukowina, the Vorarlberg, Innspruck, and Dalmatia, have each a separate popular assembly. This certainly shows a regard to national distinctions and wishes. In the Reichrath the members speak freely, criticise the policy of the government, and even demur to vote the supplies demanded. Upon the whole, this transformation of Austria from a despotic to a constitutional monarchy is one of the most remarkable and promising events of our day.

CCCXXXIII.

The Provincial System to a certain extent exists in Great Britain, for though Scotland has lost her Parliament, she has retained many other local institutions different from those of England, particularly her Law, her system of Education, and her Church. Not so Ireland. In losing her Parliament she lost all that was national. In the Imperial Legislature, England, Scotland, and Ireland are all represented, agreeably to the Provincial System.

CCCXXXIV.

The Provincial System combines, like the Federal, the Central with the Local system; the former giving the preponderance to the Central, the latter to the Local powers. Provincialism is applicable, no doubt, to a pretty extensive empire; but scarcely to a country like that of the United States embracing great part of a continent, with striking diversities of character, manners, and customs. Massachusetts, Carolina, California could never be governed as Provinces subject to a sovereign power at Washington.

THE COLONIAL SYSTEM.

CCCXXXV.

One other system of government remains to be noticed, combining Central with Local jurisdiction, namely the Colonial.

CCCXXXVI.

This is the system suited to the relation which a Colony bears to the Mother Country; and it is exemplified on a large scale in the Colonial Empire of Great Britain.

CCCXXXVII.

This system agrees with the Provincial, inasmuch as each of the Colonies is supposed to have local institutions, particularly a Colonial Legislature, not sovereign, but dependent on the Mother Country; while it differs from the Provincial in this, that the Colony is not represented in the Imperial Parliament.

CCCXXXVIII.

Consequently the Colony is really subject to the Mother Country, and what liberties it enjoys are held entirely at her good will and pleasure. The system then is of the nature of despotism, but modified by sufferance.

CCCXXXIX.

Accordingly, the Colonial institutions may be changed, suspended, or suppressed without the consent of the Colony, solely at the will of the Mother Country. Thus, not many years ago the Legislature of Jamaica was suspended, and in 1840 the Constitution of Canada was completely changed by the Imperial Parliament. In 1851 the great work of the Government of Great Britain was the framing of Constitutions for those Colonies which hitherto had not enjoyed them. These were *granted* by the Mother Country, just as the French *Charte* was *octroyée* by Louis XVIII. on the principle of divine right.

CCCXL.

The Colonial System, like the rule of a father over his children, seems suited to the infancy and growth of a Colony, but it has too much of dependence and subjection for adult age. It must then be looked upon as a temporary system, though, as compared with the youth of an individual, that of a Colony may last long. The attempt of the British Parliament to strain its prerogative by the imposition of *internal* taxes on the Colonies was, no doubt, the ostensible cause of the American war; but we can hardly suppose that States so powerful would long have submitted to be subject to Great Britain, to have no vote on the most important points, none on any Imperial questions, even on foreign and colonial trade.

CCCXLI.

When Colonies become so powerful, so full of the spirit of independence, there is but one way of inducing them to remain united to the Mother Country. This is by changing the Colonial into the Provincial System.

CCCXLII.

The cry of the American Colonies was, No Taxation without Representation, and a very fair cry it was: though they allowed the Mother Country to regulate duties paid on goods imported.

CCCXLIII.

Had then the British Parliament agreed to admit within herself Deputies from the North American Colonies, these might have remained faithful to the British Crown.

CCCXLIV.

This hint may suffice for another occasion. The admission of a number of Colonial members would, no doubt, change the character of the Imperial House of Commons; and the change might be so great as even to endanger the Constitution. The alternative would then be, modify your Constitution; or lose your Colony. We leave this for the consideration of future Statesmen and Legislators.

CONCLUSION.

These *Aphorisms* are ended. But I cannot conclude without raising a voice of indignation, weak and ineffectual though it be, a voice of intense indignation, against those Powers of Europe who have perpetrated, or allowed to be perpetrated, a political atrocity in our times. The partition of Poland has always been considered a crime in the actors, and a disgrace to those who suffered it and now, in the partition of Denmark, we witness the same crime, and the same disgrace. In permitting the partition and spoliation of this little kingdom, the Powers of Europe have not only sacrificed an interesting nation, but they have allowed a solemn treaty of only ten years standing to be torn in pieces without raising a finger to prevent it, and they have winked at the violation of that most sacred principle whereby all the Powers were supposed bound to uphold against all aggression the independence even of the smallest.

Nor was it necessary to go to war to prevent this atrocity. Had France and England together agreed to tell Austria and Prussia that the passing of the Eyder would be looked upon as a *casus belli*, the invasion of Sleswig never would have taken place; had England alone declared the same, in all probability that river never would have been crossed. Where then was that voice which formerly sounded throughout Europe, where was that arm which once smote the strong? That voice evaporated in empty threats, that arm fell only on the weak. Who, then, in the agony of his soul would not have exclaimed, Oh for an hour of Chatham!

23 MH 65

H. & J. Pillans, Printers, Edinburgh.

EDUCATIONAL WORKS
PRINTED FOR
WALTON AND MABERLY.

ENGLISH.

Dr. R. G. Latham. The English Language. A New Edition.
Complete in one volume. 8vo. 18s. cloth.

Latham's Elementary English Grammar, for the Use of
Schools. Nineteenth thousand. With Chapters on Parsing and Punctuation, also Exercises and Questions for Examination. Small 8vo. 4s. 6d. cloth.

Latham's Hand-book of the English Language, for the Use
of Students of the Universities and higher Classes of Schools. Fifth Edition. Small 8vo. 7s. 6d. cloth.

Latham's Smaller English Grammar for the Use of Schools.
By Dr. R. G. Latham and Miss M. C. Maberly. 3rd Ed. Fcap. 8vo., 2s. 6d. cloth.

Latham's English Grammar for Classical Schools. Third
Edition. Revised and enlarged. Fcap. 8vo. 2s. 6d. cloth.

Latham's Logic in its Application to Language.
12mo. 6s. cloth.

Mason's English Grammar; including the Principles of
Grammatical Analysis. 12mo. Second Edition. 2s. 6d.

Mason's Grammatical Analysis of Sentences. 12mo. 1s.

Mason's First Steps in English Grammar for Junior Classes.
18mo. 9d., cloth.

Mason's Goldsmith's "Traveller," with Notes on the Analysis
and a Life of Goldsmith. Crown 8vo. 1s. 6d.

Mason's Milton's "Paradise Lost." Books 1 and 2, with Notes
on the Analysis and Parsing. Crown 8vo. each 2s., cloth.

Mason's Thomson's "Spring," with Notes on the Analysis
and Parsing, and a Life of Thomson. Crown 8vo. 2s., cloth.

Mason's Thomson's "Winter," with Notes on the Analysis
and Parsing, and a Life of Thomson. Crown 8vo. 2s. cloth.

Abbott's First English Reader.
Third Edition. 12mo., with Illustrations. 1s. cloth, limp.

Abbott's Second English Reader.
Third Edition. 12mo. 1s. 6d. cloth, limp.

COMPARATIVE PHILOLOGY.

Latham's Elements of Comparative Philology.
1 vol. 8vo. £1 1s.

GREEK.

Kühner's New Greek Delectus; being Sentences for Trans-
lation from Greek into English, and English into Greek; arranged in a systematic Progression. By the late Dr. Alexander Allen. Seventh Edition. 12mo. 4s.

Greenwood's Greek Grammar, including Accidence, Irre-
gular Verbs, and Principles of Derivation and Composition; adapted to the System of Crude Forms. Second Edition. Small 8vo. 5s. 6d. cloth.

Gillespie's Greek Testament Roots, in a Selection of Texts,
giving the power of Reading the whole Greek Testament without difficulty. With Grammatical Notes, and a Parsing Lexicon associating the Greek Primitives with English Derivatives. Post 8vo. 7s. 6d. cloth.

Robson's Constructive Exercises for Teaching the Elements
of the Greek Language, on a system of Analysis and Synthesis, with Greek Reading Lessons and copious Vocabularies. 12mo., pp. 408. 7s. 6d. cloth.

The London Greek Grammar. Designed to exhibit, in
small Compass, the Elements of the Greek Language. Sixth Edition. 12mo. 1s. 6d.

Smith's Plato. The Apology of Socrates, the Crito, and
part of the PHAEDO; with Notes in English from Stallbaum, Schleiermacher's Introductions, etc. Edited by Dr. WM. SMITH, Editor of the Dictionary of Greek and Roman Antiquities, &c. Fourth Edition. 12mo. 5s. cloth.

Hardy and Adams's Anabasis of Xenophon. Expressly for
Schools. With Notes, Index of Names, and a Map. 12mo. 4s. 6d. cloth.

LATIN.

New Latin Reading Book; consisting of Short Sentences,
Easy Narrations, and Descriptions, selected from Caesar's Gallic War; in Systematic Progression. With a Dictionary. Third Edition, revised. 12mo. 2s. 6d.

Allen's New Latin Delectus; being Sentences for Transla-
tion from Latin into English, and English into Latin; arranged in a systematic Progression. Fourth Edition, revised. 12mo. 4s. cloth.

The London Latin Grammar; including the Eton Syntax
and Prosody in English, accompanied with Notes. Sixteenth Edition. 12mo. 1s. 6d.

Robson's Constructive Latin Exercises, for teaching the
Elements of the Language on a System of Analysis and Synthesis; with Latin Reading Lessons and Copious Vocabularies. Fourth Edition. 12mo. 4s. 6d.

Robson's First Latin Reading Lessons. With Complete
Vocabularies. Intended as an Introduction to Caesar. 12mo. 2s. 6d. cloth.

Smith's Tacitus; Germania, Agricola, and First Book of
the ANNALS. With English Notes, original and selected, and Bötticher's remarks on the style of Tacitus. Edited by Dr. WM. SMITH, Editor of the Dictionary of Greek and Roman Antiquities, etc. Third Edition, greatly improved. 12mo. 5s.

Terence. Andria. With English Notes, Summaries, and
Life of Terence. By NEWENHAM TRAVERS, B.A., late Assistant-Master in University College School. Fcap. 8vo. 3s. 6d.

BIBLICAL ILLUSTRATION.

The Englishman's Hebrew and Chaldee Concordance of the
Old Testament, being an attempt at a verbal connexion between the Original and the English Translation, with Indexes, a List of Proper Names, and their occurrences. Second Edition, revised. 2 Volumes, Royal 8vo. £3 13s. 6d. cloth.

The Englishman's Greek Concordance of the New Testament.
Third Edition. Royal 8vo. £2 2s.

HEBREW.

Hurwitz' Grammar of the Hebrew Language. Fourth Edition. 8vo. 13s. cloth. Or in Two Parts, sold separately:—ELEMENTS. 4s. 6d. cloth. ETYMOLOGY and SYNTAX. 9s. cloth.

FRENCH.

Merlet's French Grammar. By P. F. Merlet, Late Professor of French in University College, London. New Edition. 12mo. 5s. 6d. bound. Or sold in Two Parts —PRONUNCIATION and ACCIDENCE, 3s. 6d.; SYNTAX, 3s. 6d.

Merlet's Le Traducteur; Selections, Historical, Dramatic, and MISCELLANEOUS, on a plan to render reading and translation peculiarly serviceable in acquiring the French Language; 14th Edit. 12mo. 5s. 6d.

Merlet's Exercises on French Composition. Extracts from English Authors to be turned into French; Notes indicating the Differences in Style between the two Languages. Idioms, Mercantile Terms, Correspondence, etc. 12mo. 3s. 6d.

Merlet's French Synonymes, explained in Alphabetical Order. Copious Examples. 12mo. 2s. 6d.

Merlet's Aperçu de la Litterature Française. 12mo. 2s. 6d.

Merlet's Stories from French Writers; in French and English Interlinear (from Merlet's "Traducteur"). Second Edition. 12mo. 2s.

ITALIAN.

Smith's First Italian Course; being a Practical and Easy Method of Learning the Elements of the Italian Language. Edited from the German of FILIPPI, after the method of Dr. AHN. 12mo. 3s. 6d. cloth.

INTERLINEAR TRANSLATIONS.

Locke's System of Classical Instruction. Interlinear TRANSLATIONS. 1s. 6d. each.

Latin.
Phaedrus's Fables of Æsop.
Virgil's Æneid. Book I.
Caesar's Invasion of Britain.

Greek.
Homer's Iliad. Book I.
Herodotus's Histories. Selections.

French.
Sismondi; the Battles of Cressy and Poictiers.

Also, to accompany the Latin and Greek Series.

The London Latin Grammar. 12mo. 1s. 6d.
The London Greek Grammar. 12mo. 1s. 6d.

HISTORY, MYTHOLOGY, ANTIQUITIES, Etc.

A History of the World, from the Earliest Records to the Present Time, in one continuous narrative. By PHILIP SMITH, B.A., one of the principal contributors to Dr. Smith's Classical Dictionaries. The Work will form 8 vols. 8vo., illustrated by Maps and Plans, divided as follows, each division complete in itself:—

ANCIENT HISTORY. 3 vols. (*Vols. 1 and 2 now Ready.*)
MEDIEVAL HISTORY. 1 vol.
MODERN HISTORY. 4 vols.

In Monthly Parts, at 2s.; and Half-Yearly Volumes.

⁎⁎ Parts 1 to 13 *Now Ready* (Dec. 1, 1864.) *Also Vols.* 1 *and* 2, *each* 12s. 6d.

Creasy's (Professor) History of England. With Illustrations.
One Volume. Small 8vo. Uniform with Schmitz's "History of Rome," and Smith's "History of Greece." (In the Press).

Smith's Smaller History of England. With Illustrations.
Fcap. 8vo. 3s. 6d.

Schmitz's History of Rome, from the Earliest Times to the Death of Commodus, A.D. 192. Ninth Edition. 100 Engravings. 12mo. 7s. 6d.

Smith's Smaller History of Rome. With 79 Illustrations.
Fcap. 8vo. 3s. 6d. cloth.

Smith's History of Greece, from the Earliest Times to the Roman Conquest. New Edition. 100 Engravings. Large 12mo. 7s. 6d.

Smith's Smaller History of Greece. With Illustrations.
Fcp. 8vo. 3s. 6d. cloth.

Smith's Dictionary of the Bible. By various Writers. With Illustrations. Three Volumes. Medium 8vo. £5 5s.

Smith's Dictionary of Greek and Roman Antiquities. By various Writers. Second Edition. With Illustrations. 1 vol. 8vo. £2 2s.

Smith's Smaller Dictionary of Greek and Roman Antiquities. Abridged from the larger Dictionary. New Edition. Crown 8vo. 7s. 6d.

Smith's Dictionary of Greek and Roman Biography and Mythology. By various Writers. With Illustrations. 3 vols. 8vo. £5 15s. 6d.

Smith's Classical Dictionary of Biography, Mythology, and Geography. Fifth Edition. 750 Illustrations. 8vo. 18s. cloth.

Smith's Smaller Classical Dictionary of Biography, Mythology, and Geography. 200 Engravings on Wood. Crown 8vo. 7s. 6d.

Smith's Dictionary of Greek and Roman Geography. By various Writers. Illustrated with Woodcuts. Two Volumes 8vo. £4 cloth.

Ancient Rome. By T. H. Dyer. Reprinted from the "Dictionary of Greek and Roman Geography." With a Map of Ancient Rome, and 50 Illustrations. Large 8vo. 7s. 6d. cloth.

Niebuhr's History of Rome. Translated by Bishop Thirlwall, Archdeacon Hare, Dr. Smith, and Dr. Schmitz. Three Vols. 8vo. £1 16s.

Newman (F.W.) The Odes of Horace. Translated into Unrhymed Metres, with Introduction and Notes. Crown 8vo. 5s. cloth.

Newman (F.W.) The Iliad of Homer. Faithfully translated into Unrhymed Metre. 1 vol. crown 8vo. 6s. 6d. cloth.

Akerman's Numismatic Manual, or Guide to the Collection and Study of Greek, Roman, and English Coins. Many Engravings. 8vo. £1 1s.

MENTAL PHILOSOPHY.

Ramsay's (Sir George) Principles of Psychology. 8vo. 10s. 6d.

Ramsay's (Sir George) Instinct and Reason; or, the First Principles of Human Knowledge. Crown 8vo. 5s. cloth.

PURE MATHEMATICS.

De Morgan's Elements of Arithmetic. Eighteenth Thousand. Royal 12mo. 5s. cloth.

Ellenberger's Course of Arithmetic, as taught in the Pestalozzian School, Worksop. Post 8vo. 6s. cloth.
*** The Answers to the Questions in this Volume are now ready, price 1s. 6d.

Reiner's Lessons on Form; An Introduction to Geometry, as given in a Pestalozzian School, Cheam, Surrey. 12mo. 3s. 6d.

Reiner's Lessons on Number, as given in a Pestalozzian School, Cheam, Surrey. Master's Manual, 5s.

Table of Logarithms Common and Trigonometrical to Five Places. Under the Superintendence of the Society for the Diffusion of Useful Knowledge. Fcap. 8vo. 1s. 6d.

Four Figure Logarithms and Anti-Logarithms on a Card. 1s.

Barlow's Table of Squares, Cubes, Square Roots, Cube Roots, and Reciprocals of all Integer Numbers, up to 10,000. Royal 12mo. 8s.

MIXED MATHEMATICS.

Potter's Treatise on Mechanics, for Junior University Students. By RICHARD POTTER, M.A., Professor of Natural Philosophy in University College, London. Fourth Edition. 8vo. 8s. 6d.

Potter's Treatise on Optics. Part I. All the requisite Propositions carried to First Approximations, with the construction of Optical Instruments, for Junior University Students. Second Edition. 8vo. 9s. 6d.

Potter's Treatise on Optics. Part II. The Higher Propositions, with their application to the more perfect forms of Instruments. 8vo. 12s. 6d.

Potter's Physical Optics; or, the Nature and Properties of Light. A Descriptive and Experimental Treatise. 100 Illustrations. 8vo. 6s. 6d.

Newth's Elements of Mechanics, including Hydrostatics, with numerous Examples. By SAMUEL NEWTH, M.A., Fellow of University College, London. Third Edition. Revised and Enlarged. Small 8vo. 8s. 6d. cloth.

Newth's First Book of Natural Philosophy; or, an Introduction to the Study of Statics, Dynamics, Hydrostatics, and Optics, with numerous Examples. 12mo. 3s. 6d. cloth.

Newth's Mathematical Examples. A graduated series of Elementary Examples, in Arithmetic, Algebra, Logarithms, Trigonometry, and Mechanics. Crown 8vo. With Answers. 8s. 6d. cloth.
Sold also in separate Parts, without Answers:—

Arithmetic, 2s. 6d.	Trigonometry and Logarithms, 2s. 6d.
Algebra, 2s. 6d.	Mechanics, 2s. 6d.

NATURAL PHILOSOPHY, CHEMISTRY, Etc.

Lardner's Museum of Science and Art. Complete in 12
Single Volumes, 18s., ornamental boards; or 6 Double Ones, £1 1s., cl. lettered.
*** *Also, handsomely half-bound morocco, 6 volumes, £1 11s. 6d.*

CONTENTS:—The Planets; are they Inhabited Worlds? Weather Prognostics. Popular Fallacies in Questions of Physical Science. Latitudes and Longitudes. Lunar Influences. Meteoric Stones and Shooting Stars. Railway Accidents. Light. Common Things.—Air. Locomotion in the United States. Cometary Influences. Common Things.—Water. The Potter's Art. Common Things.—Fire. Locomotion and Transport, their Influence and Progress. The Moon. Common Things.—The Earth. The Electric Telegraph. Terrestrial Heat. The Sun. Earthquakes and Volcanoes. Barometer, Safety Lamp, and Whitworth's Micrometric Apparatus. Steam. The Steam Engine. The Eye. The Atmosphere. Time. Common Things.—Pumps. Common Things.—Spectacles—The Kaleidoscope. Clocks and Watches. Microscopic Drawing and Engraving. The Locomotive. Thermometer. New Planets.—Leverrier and Adams's Planet. Magnitude and Minuteness. Common Things.—The Almanack. Optical Images. How to Observe the Heavens. Common Things.—The Looking Glass. Stellar Universe. The Tides. Colour. Common Things.—Man. Magnifying Glasses. Instinct and Intelligence. The Solar Microscope. The Camera Lucida. The Magic Lantern. The Camera Obscura. The Microscope. The White Ants; their Manners and Habits. The Surface of the Earth, or First Notions of Geography. Science and Poetry. The Bee. Steam Navigation. Electro-Motive Power. Thunder, Lightning, and the Aurora Borealis. The Printing-Press. The Crust of the Earth. Comets. The Stereoscope. The Pre-Adamite Earth. Eclipses. Sound.

Lardner's Animal Physics, or, the Body and its Functions
familiarly Explained. 520 Illustrations. Uniform with the "Museum of Science and Art." 2 vols., small 8vo. each 3s. 6d. cloth lettered.

Dr. Lardner's Popular Series of Papers from the
"Museum of Science and Art," arranged according to subjects. Each subject, or group of subjects, illustrated by Engravings on Wood, complete in itself, with a Title and Wrapper, price 6d.

How to observe the Heavens—The New Planets—Leverrier and Adams's Planet Astronomical Instruments. 6d.
Steam and Steam Engine. 6d.
Time, its Measure and Reckoning Explained. 6d.
The Microscope. 6d.
Clocks and Watches — Electromotive Power. 6d.
The Electric Telegraph (Treble Number). 1s. 6d.
The Almanack Explained. 6d.
The Planets; are they Inhabited Worlds? 6d.
The Potter's Art. 6d.
First Notions of Geology (Double Number.) 1s.
Comets and Cometary Influences. 6d.
Microscopic Drawing and Engraving. 6d.
The Pre-Adamite Earth. (Double Number.) 1s.
Earth, Air, Fire and Water. 6d.
The Locomotive: Railway Accidents. 6d.
The Eye, Magnifying Glasses, Spectacles and Kaleidoscope. 6d.

Sun, Moon, Latitudes and Longitudes, and Tides. 6d.
Thermometer, Barometer, Safety Lamp, Whitworth's Apparatus, Pumps, Printing Press. 6d.
Locomotion and Transport.—Locomotion in the United States. 6d.
Terrestrial Heat and Meteoric Stones. 6d.
Optical Images, Looking-Glasses, Stereoscope. 6d.
Magnitude and Minuteness, Science and Poetry, Popular Fallacies, Lunar Influences, Weather Prognostics. 6d.
Thunder and Lightning, Aurora Borealis, Eclipses, Atmosphere, Sound. 6d.
Light, Colour, Solar Microscope, Camera Lucida, Camera Obscura, Magic Lantern. 6d.
Steam Navigation. 6d.
The Surface of the Earth; or First Notions of Geography. 6d.
Man: The Bee and White Ants: With Instinct and Intelligence. (Treble Number.) 1s. 6d.
The Stellar Universe. 6d.

Lardner's Hand-Book of Natural Philosophy.
1334 Cuts. Complete in 4 vols. 20s.
*** Also in Volumes separately as under—
Mechanics, 5s. | Optics. 5s.
Hydrostatics, Pneumatics and Heat. 5s, | Electricity, Magnetism, & Acoustics. 5s.

Lardner and Dunkin's Hand-Book of Astronomy.
Second Edition. Revised. 35 Plates and 105 Illustrations on Wood. Complete in 1 vol., small 8vo., 7s. 6d.

Lardner's Natural Philosophy for Schools.
328 Illustrations. Third Edition. 1 vol., large 12mo., 3s. 6d. cloth.

Lardner's Animal Physiology for Schools (chiefly taken from the "Animal Physics"). 190 Illustrations. 12mo. 3s. 6d. cloth.

Glossary of Scientific Terms for General Use. By Alexander HENRY, M.D. Small 8vo., 3s. 6d.

Lardner's Popular Geology. (From "The Museum of Science and Art.") 201 Illustrations. 2s. 6d.

Lardner's Common Things Explained. Containing: Air—Earth—Fire—Water—Time—The Almanack—Clocks and Watches—Spectacles—Colour—Kaleidoscope—Pumps—Man—The Eye—The Printing Press—The Potter's Art—Locomotion and Transport—The Surface of the Earth, or First Notions of Geography. (From "The Museum of Science and Art.") With 233 Illustrations. Complete, 5s., cloth lettered.
*** Sold also in Two Series, 2s. 6d. each.

Lardner's Popular Physics. (From "The Museum of Science and Art.") With 85 Illustrations. 2s. 6d. cloth lettered.

Lardner's Popular Astronomy. (From "The Museum of Science and Art.") 182 Illustrations. Complete, 4s. 6d. cloth lettered.
*** Sold also in Two Series, 2s. 6d. and 2s. each.

Lardner on the Microscope. (From "The Museum of Science and Art.") 1 vol. 147 Engravings. 2s.

Lardner on the Bee and White Ants; their Manners and Habits; with Illustrations of Animal Instinct and Intelligence. (From "The Museum of Science and Art.") 1 vol. 135 Illustrations. 2s., cloth lettered.

Lardner on Steam and its Uses; including the Steam Engine and Locomotive, and Steam Navigation. (From "The Museum of Science and Art.") 1 vol., with 89 Illustrations. 2s.

Lardner on the Electric Telegraph.
100 Illustrations. (From "The Museum of Science and Art.") 12mo., 250 pages. 2s., cloth lettered.

Liebig's Natural Laws of Husbandry. 8vo. 10s. 6d.

Liebig's Letters on Modern Agriculture. Small 8vo. 6s.

Liebig's Familiar Letters on Chemistry. Fourth Edition, Enlarged. Small 8vo., 7s. 6d.

A Guide to the Stars for every Night in the Year. In Eight Planispheres. With an Introduction. 8vo. 5s., cloth.

LOGIC.

De Morgan's Formal Logic; or, the Calculus of Inference, Necessary and Probable. 8vo. 6s. 6d.

De Morgan's Syllabus of a proposed System of Logic. 8vo. 1s.

Neil's Art of Reasoning; a Popular Exposition of the Principles of Logic, Inductive and Deductive; with an Introductory Outline of the History of Logic, and an Appendix on recent Logical Developments, with Notes. Crown 8vo. 4s. 6d., cloth.

ENGLISH COMPOSITION.

Neil's Elements of Rhetoric; a Manual of the Laws of Taste, including the Theory and Practice of Composition. Crown 8vo. 4s. 6d., cl.

DRAWING.

Lineal Drawing Copies for the earliest Instruction. Comprising upwards of 200 subjects on 24 sheets, mounted on 12 pieces of thick pasteboard, in a Portfolio. By the Author of "Drawing for Young Children." 5s. 6d.

Easy Drawing Copies for Elementary Instruction. Simple Outlines without Perspective. 67 subjects, in a Portfolio. By the Author of "Drawing for Young Children." 6s. 6d.

Sold also in Two Sets.
Set I. Twenty-six Subjects mounted on thick pasteboard, in a Portfolio. 3s. 6d.
Set II. Forty-one Subjects mounted on thick pasteboard, in a Portfolio. 3s. 6d.
The copies are sufficiently large and bold to be drawn from by forty or fifty children at the same time.

SINGING.

The Singing Master. Containing First Lessons in Singing, and the Notation of Music; Rudiments of the Science of Harmony; The First Class Tune Book; The Second Class Tune Book; and the Hymn Tune Book. Sixth Edition. 8vo. 6s., cloth lettered.

Sold also in Five Parts, any of which may be had separately.

I.—*First Lessons in Singing and the Notation of Music.* 8vo. 1s.

II.—*Rudiments of the Science of Harmony or Thorough* Bass. 8vo. 1s.

III.—*The First Class Tune Book. Thirty Single and* Pleasing Airs, with suitable words for young children. 8vo. 1s.,

IV.—*The Second Class Tune Book. Vocal Music for* youth of different ages, and arranged (with suitable words) as two or three-part harmonies. 8vo. 1s. 6d.

V.—*The Hymn Tune Book. Seventy popular Hymn and* Psalm Tunes, arranged with a view of facilitating the progress of Children learning to sing in parts. 8vo. 1s. 6d.

www.ingramcontent.com/pod-product-compliance
Lightning Source LLC
Chambersburg PA
CBHW081325090426
42737CB00017B/3039